Happy Cooking, Megan
love margaret and M

two raw sisters

ALL EATERS WELCOME

BATEMAN BOOKS

Text © Rosa and Margo Flanagan 2020

Published in 2020 by David Bateman Ltd
Unit 2/5 Workspace Drive, Hobsonville, Auckland 0618, New Zealand
www.batemanbooks.co.nz

ISBN 978-1-98-853843-3

Food images by Margo Flanagan
Lifestyle images by Malia Rose Photography
Book design: Cheryl Smith, Macarn Design
Printed in China through Asia Pacific Offset Ltd

CONTENTS

WELCOME TO THE TWO RAW SISTERS!

Like many people, we've had our struggles. We've come through personal health issues like chronic fatigue and battles with being an under-weight élite athlete. This book will let you into some of the secrets of how we have changed up our lifestyles. Our mission is to educate, influence and inspire you on the importance of eating plant-based food. Whether you're gluten-free, dairy-free, vegan, a huge meat-eater, pescatarian three days a week and vegetarian the other four days, this cookbook has something for you. All eaters are welcome!

Neither of us is vegan or vegetarian, and we love all kinds of food. But we are firm believers in creating a lifestyle based around eating a majority of plants and whole, unprocessed raw ingredients. We are *real*, and pride ourselves on having a unique approach to plant-based living. We share this with you in the following pages of 90+ of our favourite recipes.

Most people start their meals with meat, with vegetables added on as a last-minute side. Two Raw Sisters want to inspire and encourage you to take on our definition of plant-based. This means starting your meal with your plants, and then adding the meat, dairy, fish, poultry, tofu or tempeh on the side, if you choose.

We have kept things as simple and straightforward as possible in this cookbook, using only the cost-effective, unprocessed raw ingredients you are familiar with and have at home. The twist is, we will show you new and inventive ways to make these basics taste more fun, exciting and delicious.

And it's quick and easy, with minimal meal preparation time and using few dishes! Most of the salads last 3–5 days in the fridge, making them great to make at the start of the week to have for your work lunches or quick dinners.

The Two Raw Sisters lifestyle is based on freedom. There are no rules. So we encourage you to use these recipes as a guideline. Don't feel you have to be a slave to measuring cups and spoons, have confidence and trust in yourself. Change ingredients to ones you like more, or to ones that need using or are in season. The kitchen can be a stressful place for a lot of people, due to all of the dos and don'ts around food. We will help you make it a more enjoyable and delicious place for everyone, by freeing you up and letting you be yourself!

Are you ready for a healthy, happy, sustainable life forever?

Let's cook!

Margo and Rosa x

⊙ @tworawsisters

⒡ Two Raw Sisters

www.tworawsisters.com

THE STARTER PACK

'FREE EATING' AND THE ART OF SUBSTITUTION

All eaters welcome
Every recipe is everything-free
GF, DF, VG, VEG

If you eat gluten or are gluten-free

Due to being gluten-intolerant ourselves, every recipe in this cookbook is gluten-free. With our flexible approach to cooking, all of our recipes give you two options: brown rice flakes or oats. The reason for this is that if you tolerate oats just fine, we encourage you to use them as they are a versatile and cheap pantry staple that you are likely to have already. So please don't feel like you have to go out and buy brown rice flakes and buckwheat, etc., as these are just substitutes for all our gluten-free eaters and coeliacs out there. But, if oats are not your thing, we have found that brown rice flakes are the best substitute for oats.

The same goes with any salad recipe that uses a grain you don't have or cannot tolerate. Simply swap it out for another one. Gluten-free and non-gluten-free grains are so easy to substitute for one another. Have confidence in yourself and be a smart cook. You aren't going to ruin the recipe by using brown rice over millet.

Fun fact: Oats themselves don't contain gluten; it is the contamination of being processed with other gluten-containing grains that causes most people to flare up.

If you eat dairy

Feel free to swap coconut yoghurt and nut milk for Greek yoghurt, whipped cream and dairy milk.

If you eat meat, fish and/or poultry

For most main dishes we have given recommendations on which protein would go well with that particular recipe.

PANTRY MUST-HAVES

This is an overall guide of every staple ingredient we have used in this cookbook. We are not saying you need every single item on this list in your pantry. We recommend you choose four to six staples in each section and simply substitute the grains, nuts and seeds, spices and dried fruits you don't have for ones you do have. We have highlighted with an asterisk the absolute essential must-haves that we always have in our pantries at home. We recommend you slowly build up any of these must-have ingredients that you currently don't have.

We normally have one or two grains in the pantry at a time (e.g. brown rice and millet), and then get a different grain (e.g. quinoa) when we need to restock.

Having a well-stocked pantry with all the essentials *and* those 'secret ingredients' (such as pomegranate molasses) is so important when it comes to organisation and making fast, easy delicious recipes.

Nuts + seeds

- pumpkin seeds*
- sunflower seeds
- almonds
- cashews*
- walnuts*
- chia seeds or flaxseeds*
- hemp seeds*
- sesame seeds (black + white)
- peanuts
- pinenuts

Oils + condiments

- cooking oil (avocado or rapeseed)*
- quality extra virgin olive oil*
- coconut oil*
- sesame oil*
- hemp oil
- apple cider vinegar*
- tamari*
- pomegranate molasses*
- nut butters*
- tahini*
- nutritional yeast*
- miso*

Sweeteners

- dates*
- honey*
- 100% pure maple syrup
- ripe bananas*
- coconut sugar

Grains

- brown rice flakes*
- brown rice*
- buckwheat groats/flakes
- rolled oats*
- millet*
- quinoa*
- quinoa flakes
- puffed grain (quinoa, amaranth, millet)
- pasta*

Legumes

- chickpeas*
- lentils
- black beans

Dried fruits

- goji berries*
- raisins
- figs
- cranberries

Spices + salt

- cumin powder/seeds*
- curry powder
- smoked paprika*
- sumac
- turmeric*
- ginger*
- cinnamon*
- chilli flakes
- dukkah
- flaky sea salt*
- black pepper*
- fresh garlic*
- fresh ginger*

General sweet

- cacao powder*
- desiccated/flaked coconut*
- vanilla bean paste or extract*
- hemp powder
- dark chocolate*
- baking soda*

General savoury

- capers
- coconut yoghurt*
- tinned tomatoes*
- sundried tomatoes

WHAT OILS ARE BEST TO COOK WITH + WHEN

Oils are very heat-sensitive, and once heated past their smoking point the good fats turn into bad fats. Here is a guide on which oils to use when ...

Cooking oils
Coconut oil (for those of you who don't like the taste of coconut oil, deodorised coconut oil will taste more neutral)
Avocado oil
Rapeseed oil

Non-cooking oils
Sesame oil
Hemp oil
Extra virgin olive oil

A TIP OR TWO

No baking paper
Unless stated, for most of the following recipes we do not use baking paper when we cook in the oven. This is because we have found that baking paper can make the fruit and vegetables sweat. Instead, when baking paper isn't used, the fruit and vegetables have direct heat contact with the tray and the end result is crispier and more golden brown and caramelised.

Loaf tins and cake tin measurement
For most snack and dessert recipes we use an adjustable loaf tin that extends from 16cm to 30cm. For cake and tart tins, we use a 22cm tin.

Double boiler
Fill the bottom pot of the double boiler halfway with water, and heat it over the stovetop. Place the chocolate (or coconut oil, etc.) in the top pot of the boiler. As the water heats up, it will start to melt the contents in the bowl. Using a double boiler helps prevent the contents from burning. If you do not have a shop-bought double boiler, it is easy to improvise one like we do: for the second pot just use an ovenproof bowl that is a bit smaller than the pot with the boiling water, so that it will rest on top of it. Alternatively, you can just use a microwave. To melt chocolate in a microwave, break it into small pieces, place in a heatproof bowl, and microwave for 30 seconds. Take the bowl out and give the chocolate a stir. Place the bowl back into the microwave and repeat this process

of cooking for 30 seconds, stopping, stirring and returning it to the microwave, until the chocolate is completely melted. To melt coconut oil in a microwave, put it on your highest setting for about 2 minutes, or up to 5 minutes if you are melting a bigger amount.

KITCHEN EQUIPMENT: THE TOP FIVE

Vitamix Explorian E310
A Vitamix is a high-speed blender, which makes everything incredibly smooth. A Vitamix is a significant investment, but it will literally change your life. We have had ours for seven years and have never had any issues with it. This is one of the cheaper Vitamixes, but from experience we think it is the best model. The jug size isn't too big or too small, so no matter the size of your batch it still blends.

Vegetable peelers
A vegetable peeler is something everyone probably has in the cutlery drawer. You can do lots of cool things with these little tools. Ribbons of cucumber or zucchini look so nice on a plate.

The julienne peeler is a lifesaver, and saves so much time when it comes to cutting. These are pretty cheap, and are a great all-round kitchen tool to have on hand.

Microplane
These are the most amazing graters for citrus, ginger, garlic and chocolate — a must-have in any kitchen.

Large chopping board
An essential in the kitchen. There is nothing worse than not having enough room on a chopping board — everything starts to fall off, making a mess, and you have to use more dishes by putting everything in bowls. Give yourself a big working space and use it as a plate for ingredients. Believe it or not, it causes a lot less stress in the kitchen.

Good sharp knife
Counter-intuitively, sharp knives are a lot safer than blunt ones. So make sure you always have a decent sharp knife, as it will make cutting a lot easier and more enjoyable. We use a Japanese brand called Shun: their 27cm standard chef knife. We find it the best size for an everyday knife.

THANK YOU

We are so excited to have had the opportunity to write a second book. Our first cookbook selling out before it even went into bookstores was a pretty incredible feeling for us both. Especially considering we had no idea what we were getting ourselves into. Since then Two Raw Sisters has grown in leaps and bounds. We feel so lucky being able to do what we absolutely love doing as our full-time jobs. So we want to take a moment to thank every single one of you. We couldn't have done this if it wasn't for all of your support in purchasing the cookbook, coming along to workshops, and following our adventures on Instagram! (Sorry for all the terrible singing ...)

The number of you who have come on our mission of inspiring, motivating and educating people on the benefits of eating plants and creating a healthy, happy, sustainable lifestyle is incredible. Thank you for spreading the Two Raw Sisters word. We really appreciate each message you send and every photo you share. You inspire us to keep doing what we are doing.

Thank you to Mum, Dad and Will, who once again have been so supportive in everything we do. Two Raw Sisters like to move at a fast pace, completing a project and starting on the next one straight away. We know it stresses you all out, but somehow you always stick by our side and support us no matter what. We couldn't have done it without that encouragement to keep following and chasing our dreams.

Thank you to the Two Raw Sisters team. To Dean, our manager, for keeping us on track and making sure everything is in proper English and spell-checked. To Lucy, our operations manager, aka our second mom, for trying a lot of the recipes and making sure they are all dummy-proof.

We hope you all love *All Eaters Welcome* as much as the first cookbook!

BREAKFAST

Breakfast is our favourite time of day. We have given you a range of
options that are great for those days when you are pushed for time, and
for when you can enjoy a slower-paced morning. Regardless, make sure
you enjoy every mouthful of nourishing food.

A lot of these breakfasts are designed to be made at the start of the
week or the night before. It's the best feeling when you wake up and
you know you have a delicious breakfast on hand to enjoy and kick-start
your day. Most recipes will last in the fridge for up to 5 days and develop
in flavour over time.

We love textures in our food. See the list of toppings we recommend
topping your breakfasts with below. Our go-tos that we top absolutely
everything with are goji berries, cacao nibs, hemp seeds and peanut
butter. Go crazy and have fun.

If you are gluten-free and/or dairy-free, see page 9.

Breakfast toppings

- coconut yoghurt
- goji berries
- Brazil nuts
- berries
- nut butter
- oat/nut milk
- hemp/pumpkin seeds
- walnuts
- sliced banana
- coconut chips
- cacao nibs
- honey

SPICED BANANA
FIG PORRIDGE

We like to make our porridge a little extra special. This one is full of satisfying, cosy textures: caramelised banana, thick, creamy porridge, and pops from the fig seeds and crunchy apple. This is great served warm in winter. Our favourite way to eat it is to make a big batch and store it in the fridge. Then we eat it cold throughout the week, because the flavours from the spices develop over time.

SERVES 2

Prep time: 10 minutes
Cooking time: 10 minutes

¾ cup brown rice flakes
   or rolled oats
¼ cup coconut flakes
1 ripe banana, broken into
   pieces
1 apple, roughly chopped
2 heaped tbsp coconut
   yoghurt
1½–2 cups water or nut or
   oat milk
1 tsp ground ginger
1 tsp ground cinnamon
2 tsp honey
3 figs, sliced
pinch of sea salt

Place all of the ingredients into a pot and cook over a medium heat for about 8–10 minutes, or until the porridge is at your desired consistency. You want the pieces of apple to have softened but still retain some crunch. Feel free to add more water/oat or nut milk if you prefer it to be more of a runnier porridge.

Make a big batch and store in an airtight container in the fridge, where it will keep for up to 4–5 days.

Eat cold throughout the week, or alternatively heat it up. Top with your desired toppings (see page 19).

STAPLE GRANOLA

We always have a variation of this in our pantry. It is so handy to sprinkle on top of any breakfast for a bit of crunch, or simply serve with yoghurt and fruit for something quick and easy. This recipe is a guideline — there are no rules with this! We haven't specified which grain or nuts and seeds to use. Have the confidence in yourself to add whatever you love or have in the pantry at home. For example, use oats or quinoa flakes if you don't have any puffed grain, or make it grain-free by adding more nuts, seeds or coconut chips. It is always fun tasting it at the end to see what you have created.

SERVES 6

Prep time: 10–15 minutes
Cooking time: 15 minutes

1 cup nuts
½ cup seeds
1 cup dates/dried figs,
    softened in boiling
    water for 5–10 minutes,
    then drained and
    roughly chopped
1 cup shredded coconut
1 cup puffed grain
1 tsp ground cinnamon
1 tsp ground ginger
pinch of sea salt

Optional
2 tbsp cacao nibs
¼ cup dried fruit (raisins,
    goji berries, figs,
    apricots)
½ cup hemp seeds

Preheat the oven to 160°C.

Put the nuts and seeds in a blender or food processor, and pulse a few times to roughly chop. Then add dates or figs, and pulse until loosely combined.

Put the remaining ingredients into a large bowl, along with the nut and date mix. Stir to combine. The mixture should resemble a chunky granola.

Place on a baking tray lined with baking paper, and cook for about 15 minutes, turning it over halfway.

Allow to cool, then add the cacao nibs and extra dried fruit and hemp seeds, if using.

Store in an airtight container in the pantry, where it will keep for up to 2 months.

CHOCOLATE MOUSSE

A bit of a 'naughty' breakfast some may think, but haters gonna hate! We love this for breakfast.

Cacao is the highest plant-based source of iron, and also contains caffeine, so truly is a great way to kick-start your day. The avocado creates a natural creaminess that is to die for. We love serving this with coconut yoghurt, granola and lots of peanut butter.

SERVES 2

Prep time: 5–10 minutes

1 avocado
2 ripe bananas
½ cup nut or oat or
   coconut milk
1 tsp ground cinnamon
½ cup cacao powder
good pinch of sea salt

Put all of the ingredients into a blender or food processor, and blend until smooth. Eat straight away, or put in the freezer, where it will keep for up to 4 months. When you are ready to eat, let it thaw on the bench for about 15 minutes. Top with your desired toppings (see page 19).

BANANA CLUSTERS

These clusters are so addictive. The bananas caramelise in the oven, and the end result tastes a bit like a childhood banana smoothie but with some lovely crunch from the nuts and seeds. The clusters can be broken up into smaller pieces for a granola, or bigger cracker-type pieces for more of a snack bar.

We like to keep a few in our bags for those 'hangry' moments that we are all familiar with!

SERVES 8

Prep time: 10 minutes
Cooking time: 25 minutes
Cooling time: 15 minutes

1 cup almonds, roughly
  chopped
1 cup walnuts, roughly
  chopped
1 cup sunflower seeds
1 cup pumpkin seeds
1 cup quinoa flakes
1 cup sultanas or raisins
2–3 very ripe bananas,
  mashed
1–2 tsp ground cinnamon
1 tsp ground ginger
pinch of sea salt

Preheat the oven to 180°C.

Place all of the ingredients into a large bowl. Mix until everything is well-combined.

Place the mixture onto a baking tray lined with baking paper, in a single layer. Bake for about 25 minutes, until the clusters start to become golden and firm. Allow to cool.

Store in an airtight container. The clusters will last up to 2 months.

TOFFEE APPLE OATS

This dish is super-delicious. We made it all the time when we were going through a phase where we weren't vibing bananas for breakfast. The apple and dates caramelise together to create a lovely natural sweetness, which is partnered with the creamy oats and coconut flakes. Perfect for a cold winter's morning. We love to make a big batch and store the oats in the fridge, and then eat them cold for breakfast — with all the extra toppings, of course.

SERVES 2

Prep time: 10 minutes
Cooking time: 5 minutes

1 cup brown rice flakes or
   rolled oats
2 cups nut or oat or
   coconut milk
½ cup coconut flakes
1 apple, grated
6 dates, pitted and thinly
   sliced
1 tsp ground cinnamon

Put all of the ingredients into a pot, and cook over a medium heat for 2–5 minutes, stirring regularly.

Divide into two bowls and top with your desired toppings (see page 19). Our favourites are julienned apple, a dollop of coconut yoghurt, crushed walnuts, a sprinkle of coconut sugar and a splash of oat milk.

This will keep in an airtight container in the fridge for up to 5 days.

HEMP TAHINI GRANOLA

This grain-free granola is so handy to have on hand, as it's an all-in-one! We love sprinkling it over pancakes, porridge or Bircher for a bit of extra crunch. Saves us having to reach for multiple jars of things to top our breakfasts with. It's equally delicious with milk, yoghurt and fresh fruit.

SERVES 4–5

Prep time: 10–15 minutes
Cooking time: 15 minutes
Cooling time: 10 minutes

2½ cups coconut flakes
1 cup seeds (we use
  sunflower and
  pumpkin)
¼ cup hemp powder
2 tbsp ground cinnamon
pinch of sea salt
3 tbsp coconut oil, melted
2 tbsp tahini
1 tbsp honey
¼ cup goji berries
¼ cup hemp seeds

Preheat the oven to 150°C.

Put the coconut flakes, seeds, hemp powder, cinnamon and salt into a bowl, and toss until evenly mixed.

In a small bowl whisk together the coconut oil, tahini and honey, until you have a smooth, runny paste. Pour the paste into the coconut flake mixture, and mix until everything is well-coated.

On a lined baking tray evenly spread out the granola, and bake in the oven for 12–15 minutes.

Once the coconut is golden brown, take the granola out of the oven and leave it to cool for 10 minutes. Once it is cool, toss through the goji berries and hemp seeds.

Store the granola in an airtight container in the fridge, to ensure the coconut stays crispy. This will keep for up to 2 months.

FIVE-MINUTE
BANANA-BREAD BOWLS

This idea is taken from a mug brownie. These would have to be one of the quickest, easiest and yummiest things to make. What's better than hot banana bread first thing in the morning topped with yoghurt and peanut butter?

If you were wanting a healthy chocolate-cake version, add 1 tablespoon of cacao powder and top with ice cream.

MAKES 1

Prep time: 10 minutes
Cooking time: 5 minutes

¼ cup buckwheat or
   rolled oats or brown
   rice flakes
1 ripe banana, mashed
1 tbsp almond butter
½ tsp ground cinnamon
½ tsp vanilla bean paste
   or extract
¼ tsp apple cider vinegar
pinch of sea salt

Place the buckwheat into a blender or food processor, and blend into a flour. Add the remaining ingredients, and blend until well-combined.

Place all of the banana-bread mixture in a heat-proof bowl, and microwave for 5 minutes.

Allow to cool slightly, then top with your desired toppings (see page 19).

Feel free to make a few banana-bread bowls in advance. Cover and store in the fridge, where they will keep for up to 5 days.

PEANUT BUTTER BANANA BAKE

YUM, YUM, YUM, YUM — we live off this banana bake. The infusions of peanut butter, banana, cinnamon and chocolate create an absolute delight in your mouth that is so addictive. This is designed to be made at the start of the week so you have breakfast sorted for the next 6 days. Otherwise it is a great way to feed a crowd when you have people coming around for breakfast. Out of all the breakfast recipes, you have to make this one.

SERVES 6

Prep time: 10–15 minutes
Cooking time: 30 minutes

2 flax 'eggs' (2 tbsp
   ground flaxseed mixed
   with 6 tbsp water)
2 ripe bananas, mashed
2 tbsp honey
2 tbsp peanut butter
pinch of sea salt
1 tsp ground cinnamon
1 tsp ground ginger
2 cups nut, oat or
   coconut milk
2½ cups of brown rice
   flakes or buckwheat
   flakes or rolled oats
½ cup pumpkin seeds
50g dark chocolate,
   roughly chopped
1 ripe banana, sliced
   to top

Preheat the oven to 180°C.

Place all of the ingredients, except the extra banana for topping, in a bowl, and mix well to combine.

Pour the mixture into a baking dish lined with baking paper. Top with slices of banana and cook for 30 minutes.

Remove from the oven, and eat either hot or cold.

Top with your desired toppings (see page 19).

Store any leftovers in a snap-lock container in the fridge, where they will keep for up to 7 days, or alternatively freeze portions for up to 1 month.

BANANA CHOC-CHIP PANCAKES

These are so quick: you can have these small pancakes every day of the week! Throw everything in the blender and that's it. No mixing bowls or spoons involved. The best part? Melted chunks of chocolate with every mouthful.

These make quite a few, because we like to store them in the fridge for breakfast during the week. We also love eating them like pikelets as a snack. FYI, they are delicious with a thick spread of peanut butter.

MAKES 16 PANCAKES

Prep time: 10–15 minutes
Cooking time: 12 minutes

2 cups buckwheat or
   rolled oats
2 ripe bananas, mashed
2 flax 'eggs' (2 tbsp
   ground flaxseed mixed
   with 6 tbsp water)
1 tsp ground cinnamon
1 tsp baking soda
pinch of sea salt
¼ cup dark chocolate,
   roughly chopped
coconut oil, for cooking

Place the buckwheat or rolled oats into a blender or food processor, and blend into a flour. Add the remaining ingredients, excluding the chocolate chunks and coconut oil. Blend until well-combined. Add the chocolate chunks, and fold them through the pancake mixture.

Heat a frying pan over a medium heat, and melt a teaspoon of coconut oil. Spoon about 3 tablespoons of pancake mixture into the pan for 1 pancake. Continue until you have covered the pan base.

Leave to cook for 2 minutes untouched or until the bottom has cooked. Flip the pancakes over, and cook on the other side for about 1 minute.

Once cooked, remove the pancakes from the pan and place on a plate. Top with your desired toppings (see page 19). We like topping our pancakes with coconut yoghurt, peanut butter and fresh banana.

Store any leftover pancakes in an airtight container in the fridge, where they will keep for up to 7 days. Otherwise, they are great frozen for up to 2 months; just pull them out of the freezer the night before you want to eat them.

MATCHA HEMP PORRIDGE

You have to make this. We love changing up the flavour of traditional porridge with things that are a bit jazzier. Matcha and hemp are two powerhouses that go amazingly well together combined with sweet caramelised banana and creamy coconut yoghurt. We always double this recipe and store the leftovers in the fridge for the following days. It's at its best after 2 days in the fridge, because the matcha, hemp and banana flavours have fully infused into the oats.

SERVES 2

Prep time: 5–10 minutes
Cooking time: 5 minutes

1½ cups water
1 cup brown rice flakes or
    rolled oats
2 ripe bananas, mashed
3 tbsp coconut yoghurt
2 tbsp hemp protein
1 tbsp matcha powder

Place all of the ingredients into a small pot, and cook over a medium–high heat. Stir regularly for 5 minutes, until your porridge has thickened.

Pour into a bowl, and top with your desired toppings (see page 19).

The porridge will keep in the fridge in an airtight container for up to 5 days.

CACAO COCONUT BIRCHER

Feeling like a bit of chocolatey indulgence to kick-start your day? Then this Bircher is for you. The texture of chocolatey soaked oats and coconut flakes topped with creamy coconut yoghurt and crunchy peanut butter is incredibly addictive.

SERVES 2

Prep time: 5–10 minutes

1 cup rolled oats (or ½ cup
   brown rice flakes and
   ½ cup rolled oats)
¼ cup coconut flakes
1 ripe banana, mashed
⅔ cup water
2 tbsp coconut yoghurt
2 tbsp cacao powder

Put all of the ingredients into a bowl, and mix until well-combined.

Divide the Bircher between 2 bowls, and top with your desired toppings (see page 19).

This will keep in an airtight container in the fridge for up to 5 days.

INSTANT CARROT AND APPLE BIRCHER

We always forget to soak our Bircher overnight. When that happens, we go straight to this recipe. The carrot and apple give so much natural sweetness and a fresh, crisp crunch to the Bircher. This lasts really well in the fridge, so we highly recommend making a big batch for the week — just add double the amount of lemon, as it preserves the apple and carrot.

SERVES 2

Prep time: 10–15 minutes

1 cup rolled oats (or 1 cup
   brown rice flakes, or
   ½ cup rolled oats/
   brown rice flakes and
   ½ cup coconut chips)
1 small apple, grated
1 medium carrot, grated
1–1½ cups nut or oat or
   coconut milk
2 tbsp raisins
1 tbsp chia seeds
1 tsp ground cinnamon
1 tsp ground ginger
1–2 tsp honey
juice of ½ lemon

Place all of the ingredients into a bowl. As you place the apple in the bowl, squeeze all of the apple juice over the oats.

Stir until well-combined. Depending on how juicy your apple is, you may want to add the extra ½ cup of nut or oat or coconut milk if the mixture is too dry for your liking.

Divide into 2 bowls, and top with your desired toppings (see page 19).

This will keep in an airtight container in the fridge for up to 5 days.

BANANA BERRY BAKE

Baked oats take a little bit longer than porridge, but they are so worth it! This bake is particularly delicious, because all the spices create beautiful aromas when cooking. We love to serve this warm out of the oven with coconut yoghurt, fresh banana and hemp seeds.

SERVES 2

Prep time: 15 minutes
Cooking time: 30 minutes

1 cup brown rice flakes or
    rolled oats
boiling water
1 cup frozen blueberries
½ cup pumpkin seeds
½ cup coconut flakes
2 bananas, mashed
¼ cup raisins
¼ cup nut or oat or
    coconut milk
1 heaped tsp ground
    cinnamon
1 heaped tsp ground
    ginger
pinch of salt

Preheat the oven to 180°C.

Place the brown rice flakes or rolled oats in a bowl, cover with boiling water and soak, until soft (about 5 minutes).

Add the remaining ingredients to the soaked rice flakes or oats, and mix well. Transfer the mixture to a baking dish.

Cook for 30 minutes, until golden and the banana is caramelised.

Remove from the oven. Eat the bake warm, topped with your desired toppings (see page 19). Or store in an airtight container in the fridge, where it will keep for up to 6 days.

SNACKS

We snack quite a lot, so quality, tasty snacks are always the best thing to have readily on hand. All of these snacks can be made in advance, and can be stored in the freezer for up to 3 months.

Snacks are a great way to start developing your confidence in substituting ingredients. Use the recipe quantities as a guideline and add whatever dried fruits, nuts and seeds and grains you have in the pantry or prefer.

If you are gluten-free, see page 9.

DOUBLE-CHOCOLATE TAHINI COOKIES

Legumes are not just great in savoury things, they are also amazing in baking. We have discovered that legumes create that decadent fudgy texture in cookies, brownies and cakes. It is a great way to increase the nutrients of sweet baked goods so they become a healthy, delicious everyday necessity rather than a naughty delicious treat.

MAKES 10

Prep time: 15 minutes
Cooking time: 12 minutes
Cooling time: 10 minutes

¼ cup buckwheat or
    rolled oats
1 x 400g can black beans,
    drained and rinsed
½ cup coconut sugar
¼ cup nut or oat or
    coconut milk
¼ cup cacao powder
2 tbsp tahini or nut butter
1 tsp baking powder
½ tsp sea salt
100g dark chocolate,
    roughly chopped

Preheat the oven to 180°C. Line a baking tray with baking paper, and set aside.

Put the buckwheat or rolled oats into a blender or food processor, and blend into a fine flour.

Add all of the remaining ingredients, except the dark chocolate, to the blender or food processor, and blend until you have a thick, smooth mixture. Mix the dark chocolate into the mixture with a spoon, until evenly distributed.

Spoon dollops of mixture onto the baking tray. With the back of a spoon, shape the dollops into cookie shapes.

Place in the oven for 12 minutes.

Once cooked, remove from the oven, and leave to cool for 10 minutes.

Store in an airtight container in the fridge, where they will keep for up to 1 week.

CASHEW CHOCOLATE THICK SHAKE

This thick shake is heavenly. Sweet banana blended with creamy avocado, bitter cacao, cashew butter and delicate vanilla. It is so good you won't believe it's made with 100% whole unprocessed ingredients.

SERVES 2

Prep time: 10 minutes

2 sliced and frozen
    bananas
1 cup nut or oat or
    coconut milk
½ avocado
½ cup cacao powder
2 tbsp cashew butter (or
    any other nut butter)
1 tsp vanilla bean paste or
    extract
pinch of sea salt

Place all of the ingredients into a blender or food processor, and blend until smooth.

Divide into 2 cups, and drink immediately.

AFGHANS

Afghans would have to be one of our favourite cookies. Half the reason for this is all of the memories of eating the walnut on top first, followed by a little bit of icing, but leaving enough to go with the cookie. We're sure most of you will relate. We know you will love these.

MAKES 12

Prep time: 25 minutes
Cooking time: 12 minutes
Cooling time: 20 minutes

Biscuits

2 cups rolled oats or
   buckwheat
¼ cup walnuts
2 cups cornflakes, crushed
   with your hands
½ cup coconut oil, melted
½ cup cacao powder
½ cup coconut sugar
½ tsp baking powder
pinch of sea salt
water, if needed

Icing

4 tbsp cashew butter
1 tbsp coconut oil, melted
1 tbsp cacao powder
1 tsp 100% pure maple
   syrup

walnuts, roughly
   chopped, to garnish

Preheat the oven to 180°C. Line a baking tray with baking paper, and set aside.

Put the oats and walnuts into a blender or food processor, and blend into a fine flour. Put into a bowl with the crushed cornflakes.

In another bowl, put the coconut oil, cacao powder, coconut sugar, baking powder and salt. Whisk until most of the sugar has dissolved.

Add the chocolate liquid to the flour, and mix until well-combined. If the mixture is too dry, add water.

Roll into balls (about 2 tablespoons per biscuit), place on the lined baking tray, and slightly flatten the balls with the back of your hand or the back of a spoon. Repeat this until all of the cookie dough is used up.

Place in the oven for 12 minutes.

Once baked, remove from the oven and allow to cool. In the meantime, make the icing.

Place all of the icing ingredients into a small bowl, and mix until well-combined.

When the biscuits are cool, top with the icing and chopped walnuts.

Store in an airtight container in the fridge, where they will keep for up to 2 weeks.

BANANA CHOCOLATE-CHUNK BREAD

Isn't banana bread just the best? This one is an improved version from cookbook #1, with the addition of crunchy, earthy walnuts and chocolate chunks. We love having a thick slice spread with peanut butter.

MAKES 1 LOAF

Prep time: 15 minutes
Cooking time: 45 minutes
Cooling time: 20 minutes

2 cups buckwheat or
   rolled oats
4 ripe bananas, mashed
2 flax 'eggs' (2 tbsp
   ground flaxseed mixed
   with 6 tbsp water)
½ cup walnuts, roughly
   chopped
½ cup dark chocolate,
   roughly chopped
1 tsp baking soda
1 tsp apple cider vinegar

Preheat the oven to 180°C. Line a loaf tin with baking paper, and set aside.

Put the buckwheat into a blender or food processor, and blend until a fine flour is formed.

Place the buckwheat flour into a large bowl, along with all of the remaining ingredients. Mix until well-combined.

Pour the banana-bread mixture into the loaf tin. Spread the mixture evenly, and flatten with the back of a spoon or spatula.

Place in the oven to cook for 45 minutes.

Once cooked, remove from the oven, and allow to cool.

Remove from the loaf tin, and store in an airtight container, where it will keep for up to 5 days.

CHOCOLATE AND TAHINI FLAPJACKS

Flapjacks were a lunchbox staple back in the schooldays. We have made these ones a little more decadent and delicious, with the addition of tahini and chocolate. Expect creamy, salty, honey-coated oats with a layer of melt-in-your-mouth chocolate. Mixing tahini with chocolate makes it creamier, like a ganache. It cuts a lot more easily, too, so you don't get cracks when you cut it.

MAKES 10

Prep time: 15 minutes
Cooking time: 5 minutes
Setting time: 2 hours

Base

2 cups rolled oats
½ cup coconut oil, melted
3 tbsp honey
1 tbsp tahini
1 tsp ground cinnamon
pinch of sea salt

Chocolate top

100g dark chocolate,
   roughly broken
3 tbsp tahini
1 tsp vanilla bean paste or
   extract
pinch of sea salt
1 tbsp 100% pure maple
   syrup (optional)

hemp seeds or sesame
   seeds (optional)

Place all of the base ingredients into a medium-sized bowl, and mix until the ingredients are well-combined and stick together nicely.

Line a tin with a beeswax wrap or cling film, and evenly press the base mixture into the tin. Smooth it out with the back of a spoon to get a flat finish. Place in the freezer while you make the chocolate top.

Melt the chocolate using a double boiler, and then add the rest of the chocolate top ingredients. Whisk together until silky smooth.

Remove the tin from the freezer, and pour the chocolate over the base, spreading it evenly. Sprinkle with the hemp or sesame seeds, if you are using them.

Place the tin back in the freezer to set for a minimum of 2 hours.

Remove from the freezer, and cut into bars.

Store in the fridge or freezer in an airtight container. These will last in your fridge for up to 2 weeks, and in your freezer for 2 months.

PB + J MUFFINS

These are great for lunchboxes because they're an all-in-one — banana bread with peanut butter and jam enclosed within — so there's no need to take jars of peanut butter and jam with you to work or school. We also love having a couple for breakfast on the go.

MAKES 12

Prep time: 15–20 minutes
Cooking time: 20 minutes
Cooling time: 15 minutes

2 cups buckwheat or
    rolled oats
3 large ripe bananas
¾ cup nut or oat or
    coconut milk
¼ cup peanut butter
1 tbsp apple cider vinegar
1 tsp baking soda
1 tsp vanilla bean paste or
    extract
pinch of sea salt

Filling
6 tsp peanut butter
6 tsp raspberry jam, plus
    extra to top

Preheat the oven to 190°C.

Grease a muffin tin with melted coconut oil. (Dip a corner of a paper towel in the melted coconut oil, then spread it evenly in each hole.) Set aside.

Place the buckwheat or rolled oats into a blender or food processor, and blend until a fine flour is formed. Add all of the remaining ingredients, and blend until smooth.

Fill each muffin hole halfway up with the mixture. Place ½ teaspoon of peanut butter and ½ teaspoon of jam into each muffin. Cover to the top with the leftover mixture. Add an extra dollop of jam to the top of each muffin, and swirl into the mixture with a skewer or a toothpick.

Bake for 20 minutes, or until a toothpick inserted in the centre comes out clean.

Remove from the oven, and allow to cool, before removing the muffins from the muffin tray.

These will store in an airtight container in the fridge, where they will keep for up to 7 days, or in the freezer for up to 2 months.

CHOCOLATE-CHIP BANANA-BREAD BALLS

These are little morsels of delicious raw banana-bread cookie dough with chunks of crunchy chocolate. They are a super cost-effective snack made with our key pantry staples — and the only thing to wash up is the blender or food processor.

Instead of making a banana cake to use up old brown bananas, make a big batch of these. They last in the freezer for 3 months!

SERVES 12

Prep time: 15 minutes
Setting time: 30 minutes

1¼ cups brown rice flakes
    or rolled oats
1 cup desiccated coconut
1 ripe banana, peeled
3 tbsp honey
1 tbsp tahini or nut butter
½ tsp ground cinnamon
½ tsp vanilla bean paste
    or extract
pinch of sea salt
50g dark chocolate,
    roughly chopped

Place the brown rice flakes and coconut into a blender or a food processor, and blend until a flour is formed.

Add the remaining ingredients, except for the chocolate, and blend until the mixture forms a dough. Stir through the chocolate chunks.

Use your hands to press and shape the dough into balls. Alternatively, you can line a slice tin with baking paper and press the dough into the tin. Flatten with the back of a spoon to create a smooth, flat surface. Place the balls or the slice in the freezer to set for at least 30 minutes, then remove and cut the slice into bars.

Store either the balls or the bars in an airtight container in the freezer for up to 3 months.

FUDGY DOUBLE-CHOCOLATE MUFFINS

No one will ever know these have zucchini in them. The zucchini helps with the delicious fudgy consistency of the muffins. They are a great 3 o'clock pick-me-up, or we love serving them as a dessert, slightly warmed-up so the chunks of chocolate are melted, and with a scoop or two of ice cream.

MAKES 12 MUFFINS

Prep time: 15–20 minutes
Cooking time: 17 minutes
Cooling time: 15 minutes

2 cups buckwheat or
   rolled oats or spelt flour
1 cup nut or oat or
   coconut milk
2 small zucchini, grated
1 cup dates, softened
   in boiling water for
   5–10 minutes, then
   drained
⅓ cup cacao powder
1 tsp vanilla bean paste or
   extract
1 tsp apple cider vinegar
1 tsp baking soda
pinch of sea salt
70g dark chocolate,
   roughly chopped

Preheat the oven to 180°C. Grease a muffin tin with melted coconut oil. (Dip a corner of a paper towel in the melted coconut oil, then spread it evenly in each hole.) Set aside.

Place the buckwheat into a blender or food processor, and blend into a flour. Add the remaining ingredients, except for the chocolate chunks, and blend until you have a smooth batter.

Add the chocolate chunks, and fold them through the mixture with a spoon. Put about 2 tablespoons of batter into each muffin hole.

Place the muffins in the oven for 17 minutes.

Poke the muffins in the middle with a skewer or a toothpick. You want there to be a little bit of batter left on the skewer when you pull it out. Then you know they are nice and fudgy on the inside!

Remove from the oven, and allow to cool before removing the muffins from the muffin tray.

Store in an airtight container in the fridge, where they will keep for up to 7 days, or in the freezer for up to 2 months.

PEANUT BUTTER CHOCOLATE BROWNIES

This is one of our most cost-effective recipes — and it's a brownie!! Not complaining there ...

The coconut and sunflower seeds make this brownie a lot lighter and have a neutral but delicious flavour, which brings out the peanut butter and cacao. These are great as an afternoon snack or cut into chunks and mixed through vanilla ice cream to make cookies and cream.

SERVES 8–10

Prep time: 10–15 minutes
Setting time: 30 minutes

1½ cups desiccated
   coconut
1½ cups sunflower seeds
½ cup peanut butter
½ cup cacao powder
2–3 tbsp 100% pure
   maple syrup or honey
pinch of sea salt

Place the coconut and sunflower seeds into a blender or food processor. Blend past a flour, so the mixture is half nut butter, half flour.

Add the remaining ingredients, and blend until smooth.

Line a tin with baking paper. Evenly press the brownie into the tin, using the back of a spoon to get a flat finish.

Place in the freezer for 30 minutes to set.

Remove from the freezer, and cut into bars. Store in an airtight container in the freezer, where they will keep for up to 3 months.

MATCHA HEMP BARS

This is one of our favourite recipes in this cookbook. We did these for our first online workshop, and everyone raved about them. They have all of the textures and flavours nailed. Matcha and hemp are a match made in heaven — if you haven't tried them together already, you must! We also have our Matcha Hemp Porridge (page 39), which is amazing, too.

No more words needed: make them and you will get what we mean ...

MAKES 8–10 BARS

Prep time: 20 minutes
Cooking time: 5 minutes
Setting time: 2 hours

4 tbsp hemp powder
¾ cup brown rice flakes
    or rolled oats
½ cup dried figs, softened
    in boiling water for
    5–10 minutes, then
    drained
½ cup dates, softened in
    boiling water for 5–10
    minutes, then drained
½ cup nut butter
1 tsp matcha powder
1 tsp ground cinnamon
½ tsp vanilla bean paste
    or extract
pinch of sea salt

Chocolate layer
100g dark chocolate,
    roughly chopped
2 tbsp coconut oil, melted

Place all of the ingredients into a blender or food processor. Blend until well-combined and a smooth batter is formed.

Line a slice tin with cling film, baking paper or a beeswax wrap, and evenly press the mixture into the tin. Flatten the top with the back of a spoon. Place in the freezer while you make the chocolate layer.

To melt the chocolate, place it in a double boiler, then add in the coconut oil.

Remove the slice from the freezer, and pour the chocolate over the slice.

Place back in the freezer for at least 2 hours, to set.

Remove from the freezer, and cut into slices.

Store in an airtight container in the freezer, where they will keep for up to 3 months. They are best eaten straight from the freezer.

MISO CARAMEL BANANA MUFFINS

These muffins are totally gluten- and nut-free by using pumpkin seed flour. Pumpkin seed flour is super-easy to make: just blend pumpkin seeds in a blender until fine. Feel free to use oats, buckwheat or almonds instead, following the same process. The miso caramel centre is a bit of a treat. Miso gives it a lovely salty flavour, along with adding a boost of fermented goodness!

MAKES 12 MUFFINS

Prep time: 25 minutes
Cooking time: 35 minutes
Cooling time: 15 minutes

Muffins
1½ cups pumpkin seeds
2 flax 'eggs' (2 tbsp ground flaxseed mixed with 6 tbsp water)
4 ripe bananas
1 heaped tsp ground cinnamon
1 heaped tsp ground ginger
1 tsp baking powder
1 tsp apple cider vinegar

Miso caramel
1 cup dates, softened in boiling water for 5–10 minutes, then drained
2 tsp miso paste
1 tsp vanilla bean paste or extract
¼ cup water mixed with 1 tbsp coconut yoghurt

Preheat the oven to 180°C. Grease a muffin tin with melted coconut oil. (Dip a corner of a paper towel in the melted coconut oil, then spread it evenly in each hole.) Set aside.

In a blender or food processor, blend the pumpkin seeds until you have achieved a flour-like texture.

Add the flax 'eggs' and all of the remaining muffin ingredients. Blend until you have a smooth, well-combined mixture. Set the muffin mixture aside while you make the miso caramel.

For the miso caramel, put all of the ingredients into a blender, or use a stick blender and a jug. Blend until super-smooth.

Fill the muffin tins halfway with the muffin mixture, then add 1 heaped teaspoon of miso caramel, before filling the remaining half of the muffin tins with the rest of the muffin mixture.

Place in the oven and cook for 30–35 minutes.

Remove from the oven, and allow to cool, before removing the muffins from the muffin tray.

These can be stored in an airtight container in the fridge, where they will keep for up to 2 weeks.

PB JELLY + HEMP COOKIE-DOUGH COOKIES

These jam-drop cookies are delicious. Peanut-buttery, hempy cookie dough with tart raspberry jelly — yes, please!

They are equally delicious rolled into bliss balls without the raspberry jelly if you can't be bothered making it.

MAKES ABOUT 10 COOKIES

Prep time: 25 minutes
Setting time: 30 minutes

Jelly
1 cup raspberries,
    defrosted or fresh
2 tbsp chia seeds

Cookies
1 cup brown rice flakes,
    or buckwheat or rolled
    oats
½ cup hemp flour
¾ cup dates, softened
    in boiling water for
    5–10 minutes, then
    drained
⅓ cup peanut butter
4 tbsp coconut oil,
    melted
2 tbsp water
1 tsp vanilla bean paste or
    extract
pinch of sea salt

Using a blender or a stick blender and jug, blitz the raspberries up until you have a paste. Fold through the chia seeds, and leave to set while you make the cookie dough.

Place the brown rice flakes and hemp flour into a blender or food processor, and blend until you have a fine flour.

Add the remaining ingredients, and blend until you have a dough that sticks together nicely.

Line a baking tray with baking paper.

For each cookie, roll a 2-tablespoon ball of dough, and flatten it out between your hands. Place on the baking tray.

With your fingers mould a well/hole in the middle of each cookie. Make sure you don't press a hole right the way through the bottom of the cookie, otherwise the jelly will spill out. Allow about 1cm of cookie dough at the base of the cookie. Spoon a teaspoon of jelly into the well of each cookie.

Place the cookies in the fridge for about 30 minutes to set, then serve.

These cookies can be stored in an airtight container in the fridge, where they will keep for up to 1 week. Alternatively, they can be kept in the freezer for up to 3 months.

POWER CHOCOLATE

This is what you eat when you need a pick-me-up. We have made this Power Chocolate as nutrient-dense and delicious as possible. Cacao is one of the highest plant-based sources of iron, so apart from tasting delicious it is also really good for you. Hemp has all 20 essential amino acids and is really high in protein. Goji berries are extremely high in vitamin A, and coconut nectar is a good source of potassium and magnesium. We say: eat as much as you want!

SERVES 12

Prep time: 10–15 minutes
Cooking time: 15 minutes
Setting time: 40 minutes

1 cup mixed nuts or seeds, chopped
200g dark chocolate, roughly chopped
1 tsp vanilla bean paste or extract
2 tbsp hemp powder
¼ cup hemp seeds, plus extra to sprinkle on top
2 tbsp coconut nectar (or any other sweetener)
⅓ cup goji berries
pinch of sea salt

Preheat the oven to 180°C.

Place the chopped nuts or seeds onto a baking tray, and roast for about 10 minutes.

In the meantime, melt the chocolate using a double boiler. Once the chocolate is melted, add the vanilla, hemp powder, hemp seeds, coconut nectar, goji berries and salt. Continue to whisk, until a smooth, silky chocolate is formed.

Line a tin with beeswax wraps or baking paper. Sprinkle half of the nuts on the base of the tin, and pour over half of the chocolate mixture. Repeat. Lastly, sprinkle with some extra hemp seeds.

Place in the freezer for 40 minutes, to set.

Once set, remove the chocolate from the freezer, and cut into pieces.

Store the chocolate in an airtight container in the freezer, where it will keep for up to 3 months.

TOASTED ALMONDS WITH PAPRIKA AND ROSEMARY

Such a hit with everyone! While this recipe makes a lot, they will not last long. So we highly recommend doubling or tripling the recipe.

The maple syrup caramelises the almonds, and the smoked paprika gives them a lovely smoky flavour that goes so well with the rosemary. Feel free to change up the nut by using peanuts or walnuts.

We love serving these as a simple nibble when guests come over, on a platter, or roughly chopped on a salad.

MAKES 2 CUPS

Prep time: 10 minutes
Cooking time: 25 minutes
Cooling time: 20 minutes

3 tbsp coconut oil
2 cups raw whole
   almonds
4 sprigs of rosemary,
   leaves removed and
   roughly chopped, stalks
   discarded
2 tbsp 100% pure maple
   syrup
2 tbsp smoked paprika
pinch of sea salt

Preheat the oven to 160°C. Line a baking tray with a sheet of baking paper, and set aside.

Melt the coconut oil in a large pan over a medium heat. Once the oil is hot, add the nuts and rosemary, and stir until the nuts are well-coated. Keep stirring for about 2 minutes, then reduce the heat to low.

Add the maple syrup, smoked paprika and salt, and continue to stir for a further minute.

Transfer the nuts to the baking tray, spreading them out in a single layer. Put the tray in the oven, and roast the nuts for 20–25 minutes.

Remove from the oven, and allow to cool.

Store in a glass jar or an airtight container in the pantry, where they will keep for up to 3 months.

AVOCADO EDAMAME SMASH

Take your avocado smash to the next level with fried lemon rind and zesty spring onions. The combination of avocado and edamame is delicious. The avocado makes it so smooth, while the beans give it lovely texture. Great as a dip or as a spread in a sandwich. When avocados aren't in season, add another cup of edamame beans or peas.

MAKES ABOUT 2 CUPS

Prep time: 15 minutes
Cooking time: 5 minutes

1½ cups edamame beans
1 large avocado
juice of ½ a lemon, plus
    1 x 8cm strip of finely
    shaved lemon rind
4 tbsp extra virgin olive
    oil
sea salt
3 spring onions, finely
    sliced

To serve
drizzle of extra virgin olive
    oil
small handful of fresh
    herbs, roughly chopped
1–2 tbsp black sesame
    seeds

Blanch the edamame beans in hot water for about 5 minutes, then drain. Set aside a good handful for the topping.

Place the rest of the beans into a blender or food processor with the avocado, lemon juice, 2 tbsp olive oil and a good pinch of salt. Blend until almost smooth.

Heat the remaining 2 tbsp of oil in a small frying pan, and gently fry the spring onions and lemon rind for 3 minutes. Take off the heat and stir in the reserved beans, adding a pinch of salt.

Spread the smash over a plate, spoon the spring onion mix into the middle, and serve. Drizzle with extra virgin olive oil, and top with the fresh herbs and black sesame seeds.

Leftovers can be stored in an airtight container in the fridge, where they will keep for up to 2 days.

MAINS

Here, we welcome all eaters, whatever their dietary stripe. So all of these salads are great served alongside meat, fish or poultry, or are just as great as a vegetarian meal with avocado, hummus, tofu, tempeh or falafel. As we keep saying: substitute. Use whatever you have in your pantry or fridge and use vegetables that are in season. Have the confidence and the freedom in yourself to do this.

Everything doesn't have to be perfect. We are home cooks, not Michelin-star chefs. So don't feel enslaved to using measuring spoons and cups — cutting loose from using them will make the kitchen a much more fun, experimental place! It will also help you to use the following recipes as guidelines, rather than as strict step-by-step instructions.

If a salad serves six and you're only feeding two, we encourage you to make the full recipe, as it can be your lunches or dinners for the next couple of days, saving you time in the kitchen. All of these salads are designed to last in the fridge for at least 3–5 days, so there is no need to worry about them going off.

If you are gluten-free and/or eat dairy, see page 9.

QUINOA, VEGGIE ALMOND BOWL WITH TAHINI MISO DRESSING

This recipe was created when we were on holiday and needed a bowl full of nourishment. The great thing about this recipe is that it is so versatile. Use whatever grain you have, whatever veggies need using in the fridge, and whatever nuts or seeds you have.

The dressing used in this bowl is our #1 go-to and a total winner. We recommend you make a big batch of it, as it keeps well in the fridge. It is full of fermented goodies that are amazing for a healthy gut.

SERVES 2

Prep time: 20 minutes
Cooking time: 20 minutes

1 cup water
½ cup quinoa
oil
½ head of broccoli, cut into florets
1 zucchini, cut into chunks
2 spring onions, sliced

Almond crunch
½ cup flaked almonds, toasted
zest of ½ lemon and juice of ½ lemon
handful of fresh herbs, roughly
    chopped (coriander, mint, parsley)
pinch of sea salt
black pepper

Tahini miso dressing
2 tbsp tahini
1 tbsp miso
juice of 1 lemon
approx. 2 tbsp water, to achieve
    desired consistency

To serve
1 avocado, cut into cubes
handful of fresh rocket or spinach
½ cup edamame beans, blanched in
    boiling water, then drained

Put the water into a pot along with the quinoa. Bring to the boil, then reduce to a simmer and cook for 7 minutes. Remove from the heat and allow the quinoa to sit for at least 10 minutes, or until all of the excess water has been absorbed.

Heat up a frying pan, and add the oil. Add the broccoli, zucchini and spring onion. Sauté until lightly golden. Set aside.

For the almond crunch, place all of the ingredients into a small bowl, and mix to combine. Set aside.

For the dressing, mix all of the ingredients together in a cup or small bowl. Set aside.

To assemble, divide the quinoa into 2 bowls, followed by the vegetables, almond crunch, and tahini miso dressing. Then add the avocado, fresh rocket or spinach, and the edamame beans.

Store in an airtight container in the fridge, where it will keep for up to 2 weeks.

CARROT CHICKPEA QUINOA

This is a simple single-bowl salad full of delicious flavours and textures. The secret to cooking quinoa perfectly is to under-cook it slightly so that it is still slightly crunchy. You can use whatever quinoa you have: red and black will be more nutty-tasting and crunchy than white. We often make this at the start of the week for work lunches, as it lasts a good 4 days and develops in flavour over time.

We highly recommend serving this salad with our Hemp Aioli (see page 96) or tahini.

SERVES 6

Prep time: 10–15 minutes
Cooking time: 7 minutes

1 cup quinoa
2 cups water

Salad
1 bunch of spring carrots, julienned
1 bunch of spring onions, finely chopped
2 x 400g cans chickpeas, drained and rinsed
½ cup raisins
½ cup pumpkin seeds, toasted
handful of mint, roughly chopped
handful of fresh rocket

Dressing
⅓ cup olive oil
½ tsp ground cumin
½ tbsp apple cider vinegar
1 tsp honey
pinch of salt
pinch of chilli flakes

Put the quinoa and water in a saucepan, and bring to the boil. Reduce to a simmer, and cook for 7 minutes. Remove from the heat, and allow any remaining water to be absorbed.

Place all of the salad ingredients into a large bowl, along with the cooked quinoa, and toss to combine.

In a separate bowl, mix all of the dressing ingredients together. Pour it over the salad and toss gently to combine.

Serve at room temperature.

Store any leftovers in an airtight container in your fridge, where they will keep for up to 4 days.

GINGER SESAME TOFU WITH PEANUT SAUCE

Everyone loves Asian fusion, right? We certainly do. Ginger Sesame Tofu and the most amazing peanut dipping sauce are two of our favourites. They're both so simple, using pantry staples you'll all have at home. On pages 91 and 92 we give you two of our favourite go-to dishes that use both.

GINGER SESAME TOFU

SERVES 2–3

Prep time: 15 minutes
Resting time: 5–10 minutes
Cooking time: 10 minutes

300g tofu

Marinade
2 tbsp sesame oil
2 tbsp tamari
2 tbsp grated fresh ginger
2 cloves of garlic, crushed
 and finely chopped
juice of 1 lime or lemon

Preheat the oven to 220°C.

Pat the tofu in between paper towels to remove any extra moisture. Then cut the tofu into slices, about 2cm thick.

Place all of the marinade ingredients in a bowl, and mix to combine.

Add the tofu to the bowl, ensuring each slice is evenly coated with the marinade.

Ideally, if you have time allow the tofu to rest for 5–10 minutes in the marinade.

Line a baking tray with baking paper, and place the tofu onto the tray, drizzling over any remaining marinade.

Cook in the oven for 10 minutes. Once cooked, remove from the oven.

The tofu will last in your fridge in an airtight container for up to 3 days.

PEANUT SAUCE

MAKES 1 CUP

Prep time: 10 minutes

3 heaped tbsp peanut butter
3 tbsp tamari
3 tsp sesame oil
3 tbsp grated fresh ginger
2 cloves of garlic, crushed
   and roughly chopped
6 tbsp water
zest and juice of 1 lime

Place all of the ingredients into a blender, or use a stick blender and jug. Blend until well-combined.

Store any remaining sauce in a jar in the fridge, where it will keep for up to 1 week.

TOFU ROLLS

We are obsessed with these. A lot of people think rice-paper rolls are a nightmare to make, but these are really easy to whip together. The flavours from the cucumber, avocado, raw bok choy and fragrant mint are so refreshing. The addition of our Ginger Sesame Tofu with Peanut Sauce (page 88) makes these rolls unforgettable. It's the perfect collision of pungent versus fresh flavours, and of a substantial versus light meal.

SERVES 2

Prep time: 25–30 minutes

4 large rice-paper rolls or
   8 small rice-paper rolls
1 x quantity of Ginger Sesame
   Tofu (page 88)
¼ cucumber, julienned
1 small avocado, sliced
good handful of mung bean
   sprouts
2 spring onions, sliced thinly
   lengthways
1–2 heads of raw bok choy,
   thinly sliced
fresh herbs (coriander or
   mint), roughly chopped
roasted peanuts, roughly
   chopped
½ x quantity of Peanut Sauce
   (page 89)

Set up your spring roll rolling station with a bowl of hot water, a dampened cutting board, the sliced tofu, the Peanut Sauce and the rest of the ingredients.

Soak the rice-paper roll in the water for about 10 seconds. Place the rice paper on the cutting board, and load all of the fillings onto it. Top with some chopped peanuts and a drizzle of Peanut Sauce. Roll, tuck, and fold in the sides as you go. Continue with remaining rice-paper rolls.

Once done, serve with some extra Peanut Sauce.

If you are making them ahead of time, place the tofu rolls in an airtight container and store in the fridge, where it will keep for up to 2 days. Place the Peanut Sauce in a separate container, where it will last up to 1 week.

ASIAN NOODLE TOFU SALAD

This beautiful fresh salad is full of flavour, and is the perfect light but substantial meal for a summer's night.

Don't be put off by the peach: it complements all of the peanut Asian flavours so well. If peaches aren't in season, you can simply leave them out. If tofu isn't your vibe, then salmon or chicken will be just as delicious.

SERVES 2

Prep time: 20–25 minutes
Cooking time (noodles):
8–10 minutes

Noodle salad
100g soba noodles,
    cooked according to
    packet instructions
1 zucchini, julienned
handful of green beans,
    thinly sliced lengthways
½ cup edamame beans,
    blanched in boiling
    water, then drained
1 spring onion, finely
    sliced
handful of fresh mint,
    roughly chopped
1 peach, stone removed,
    and sliced
¼ cup peanuts, roasted
    and roughly chopped
2 tbsp sesame seeds

½ x quantity of Peanut
    Sauce (page 89)
1 x quantity of Ginger
    Sesame Tofu (page 88)

Place all of the noodle salad ingredients into a large bowl. Gently toss with your hands, until everything is well mixed through.

Layer onto a flat, round plate. Start with half of the noodle salad, and drizzle over half of the Peanut Sauce. Scatter on half of the Ginger Sesame Tofu. Then repeat with the remaining half of the salad, sauce and tofu. Alternatively, divide the salad between 2 separate bowls and drizzle over the sauce, then top with the tofu.

Store any leftover salad in an airtight container in the fridge, where it will keep for 2 days.

CUMIN KUMARA RICE SALAD WITH GARLIC MINT YOGHURT

We love grain-based salads like this, because they are so filling and don't take too much thinking about what else to add on the side. This is such a winner during the week, and lasts well; all you need to do is scoop it into a container. If you are making it for the week, we suggest leaving out the avocado and adding it as you need it. Delicious with salmon or lamb.

SERVES 8

Prep time: 25 minutes
Cooking time: 40 minutes

1.5kg kumara (approx. 3 large), cut into large, random chunks
2 red onions, sliced
pinch of sea salt
2 tsp ground cumin
pinch of chilli flakes
oil
1½ cups brown rice
2 tbsp tamari
3 stalks kale, finely chopped
1 x 400g can of black beans, drained and rinsed
1 avocado, cut into cubes
1 cup flaked almonds, toasted
large handful of fresh coriander, roughly chopped

Garlic mint yoghurt
½ cup coconut yoghurt
juice of 1 lemon
1 clove of garlic, crushed and roughly chopped
¼ cup packed mint leaves, roughly chopped
1 tbsp tahini
pinch of sea salt
black pepper

Preheat the oven to 200°C.

Onto 2 baking trays, place the kumara, onion, sea salt, cumin and chilli flakes, then drizzle over the oil. Toss everything until well-combined. Place the baking trays in the oven and cook for 35–40 minutes, or until the kumara and onion are soft and golden. Once cooked, remove from the oven and allow to cool slightly.

Cook the brown rice, according to the packet instructions, but adding the tamari to the water at the beginning, before you bring the rice to the boil.

To make the garlic mint yoghurt, place all of the ingredients into a blender or food processor, and blitz until smooth and creamy. Pour into a bowl and set aside.

To assemble the salad, get out a large, flat salad platter. Start with a layer of brown rice, followed by the roasted kumara and onion, then the kale, black beans, avocado, garlic mint yoghurt, almonds and coriander. Continue this process for another 1–2 layers.

This salad will last in your fridge in an airtight container for 3–4 days.

POMEGRANATE CUMIN ROASTED KUMARA + POTATOES WITH HEMP AIOLI

This will take your roast potatoes to the next level. We make this Hemp Aioli a lot, as it goes with absolutely anything and everything. Feel free to add other vegetables, such as zucchini, cauliflower, red onion, etc., to make a more all-round roast vegetable salad.

SERVES 8

Prep time: 20 minutes
Cooking time: 30 minutes

1kg kumara (preferably a mix
    of size + colour), sliced
    lengthways
500g potatoes, sliced
    lengthways
2 tsp cumin seeds
2 tbsp pomegranate molasses
oil
pinch of sea salt

1 bunch of spring carrots, cut
    lengthways

Hemp Aioli
½ cup hemp seeds
¼ cup cashews
6 tbsp hemp oil
4 tbsp apple cider vinegar
2 cloves of garlic, crushed and
    finely chopped
good pinch of sea salt
black pepper

fresh rocket
dukkah

Preheat the oven to 180°C.

Place the kumara and potatoes onto 2 baking trays. Toss through the cumin seeds, pomegranate molasses, oil and salt. Cook for 30 minutes, or until soft and golden.

On another tray, place the spring carrots, and drizzle with oil and sea salt. Toss to combine. Put in the oven for 10–15 minutes. Then remove and allow to cool.

To make the Hemp Aioli, place all of the ingredients into a blender, or use a stick blender and a jug, and blend until super-smooth and creamy.

To serve, layer up the roasted kumara, potatoes and carrots with the Hemp Aioli and the rocket. Sprinkle with dukkah to finish.

Store any leftover salad in an airtight container in the fridge, where it will keep for 2–3 days.

TAHINI MILLET BROCCOLI SALAD

Oh my goodness, this salad ... We always say a dressing makes any salad, and this is a prime example. All it is, is a grain and broccoli, but the dressing has such a punch of nutrients and flavour that it turns the salad into something easy yet insanely yummy. We love making this at the start of the week for our lunches. The dressing can be made separately for other salads, and will last in the fridge.

SERVES 2–4

Prep time: 15 minutes
Cooking time: 15 minutes

1 cup millet
2 cups water
oil
1 head of broccoli, cut into
   florets
pinch of sea salt
½ cup flaked almonds,
   toasted
1 avocado, cut into chunks
good handful of coriander,
   roughly chopped

Dressing
4 tbsp extra virgin olive oil
3 tbsp tahini
zest and juice of 1 lemon
2 tbsp nutritional yeast
1 heaped tsp miso paste
pinch of sea salt
water, to loosen

Place the millet and water into a pot, and bring to the boil. Reduce to a simmer, and cook for 10 minutes. Once cooked, remove from the heat. Allow to sit for 5–10 minutes, then fluff up the millet with a fork.

Meanwhile, heat a frying pan and add some oil. Add the broccoli florets and sea salt, and cook until nicely charred.

To make the dressing, place all of the ingredients into a small bowl, and mix well to combine.

Place the millet and the dressing into a large bowl, and mix. Add the broccoli, almonds, avocado and coriander, and toss gently to combine everything.

Store any leftover salad in an airtight container in the fridge, where it will keep for up to 4 days. The dressing will keep in the fridge for up to 3 weeks.

YAM AVOCADO TAHINI

Roasted yams are one of our favourite vegetables. This is a great salad for all times of the year because it is a great mix of roasted and fresh vegetables. The fragrant herbs, crunchy cashews and creamy dressing tie everything together beautifully. Feel free to use potatoes or kumara when yams aren't in season.

SERVES 2–4

Prep time: 20 minutes
Cooking time: 30 minutes

1 red onion, sliced into
    wedges
approx. 5 large yams, sliced
    into thick slices
oil
sea salt
fresh rocket or spinach
1 zucchini, peeled into
    ribbons
½ cup edamame beans,
    blanched in boiling water,
    then drained
1 avocado, sliced
½ cup roasted cashews,
    roughly chopped
handful of fresh mint,
    roughly chopped

Dressing
3 tbsp extra virgin olive oil
2 tbsp tahini
juice of ½ a lemon
small handful of mint
    leaves, roughly chopped
1 clove of garlic, crushed
    and finely chopped
dash of apple cider vinegar
pinch of sea salt

Preheat the oven to 195°C.

Place the onion and yams on a baking tray, drizzle with the oil, and sprinkle with salt. Toss to combine.

Place in the oven for 25–30 minutes.

To make the dressing, place all of the ingredients into a cup, and mix to combine well.

To assemble the salad, layer it on a salad platter. Start with a base of fresh rocket or spinach, followed by the roasted onion and yam, zucchini ribbons, edamame beans, avocado, cashews and mint. Then drizzle over the dressing. Continue this process for another 1–2 layers.

Store any leftover salad in an airtight container in the fridge, where it will keep for up to 2 days.

MIDDLE EASTERN LEGUME SALAD

The cheapest and easiest salad to make in this book. We always tell people to use spices and fresh herbs to create flavour rather than use packaged sauces. This recipe is a prime example of making boring canned legumes something quite delicious. Use whatever canned legumes and spices you have in the pantry, and whatever herbs are in season at the time. If you don't have preserved lemons, use the zest and juice of 1 lemon.

SERVES 4

Prep time: 15–20 minutes

1 x 400g can chickpeas,
  drained and rinsed
1 x 400g can lentils, drained
  and rinsed
¼ red onion, finely chopped
handful of coriander, roughly
  chopped
handful of mint, roughly
  chopped
2 tbsp sesame seeds
2 tbsp flaked almonds,
  toasted
smoked paprika

Dressing

2 tsp ground cumin
1 tsp ground coriander
1 clove of garlic, crushed and
  finely chopped
pinch of sea salt
2 tbsp tahini
2 tbsp extra virgin olive oil
¼ preserved lemon skin,
  finely chopped

Place the chickpeas and lentils in a bowl.

To make the dressing, place all of the ingredients in a bowl, and mix to combine.

Add the chickpeas and lentils, and mix until the legumes are evenly coated with the dressing. Add the red onion, coriander, mint, sesame seeds and almonds. Gently mix to combine evenly.

Serve immediately; although this is great to make in advance, too. To serve, sprinkle with smoked paprika.

Store any leftover salad in an airtight container in the fridge, where it will keep for up to 4 days.

CINNAMON ROASTED PUMPKIN WITH SRIRACHA YOGHURT + HERBS

Here we take the humble pumpkin and turn it into a beautiful salad with only a few components. It has all of the colours, flavours and textures. Soft, bright orange pumpkin, smooth and spicy sriracha yoghurt, chunky zesty herb dressing, and crunchy pumpkin seeds. Impress a crowd or have it for your weekday lunches.

If you can't be bothered making the herb dressing in a blender, just roughly chop the herbs and mix everything in a bowl. Delicious.

SERVES 4

Prep time: 20–25 minutes
Cooking time: 25 minutes

1.2kg pumpkin, cut into
  slices
1 red onion, cut into
  chunks
½ tsp ground cinnamon
oil
¼ cup pumpkin seeds,
  toasted
large handful of fresh
  coriander, roughly
  chopped
pinch of chilli flakes

Sriracha yoghurt
½ cup coconut yoghurt
2 tsp sriracha sauce
pinch of sea salt

Herb dressing
good handful of fresh
  coriander, roughly
  chopped
4 tbsp extra virgin olive oil
juice of ½ lemon
pinch of sea salt
black pepper

Preheat the oven to 220°C.

Place the slices of pumpkin and the red onion on a baking tray, and sprinkle over the cinnamon and drizzle over the oil. Give everything a good toss to combine.

Place in the oven to cook for 20 minutes. Then turn the oven onto grill, and cook for a further 5 minutes.

To make the sriracha yoghurt, put the coconut yoghurt in a cup, along with the sriracha sauce and sea salt, and mix to combine well. Set aside.

To make the herb dressing, place all of the ingredients into a blender, and blitz to combine. Set aside.

To assemble, layer the roasted pumpkin slices and red onion on the bottom of a flat salad plate. Dollop over the sriracha yoghurt, followed by the herb dressing. Sprinkle over the toasted pumpkin seeds, coriander and chilli flakes.

Store any leftover salad in an airtight container in the fridge, where it will keep for up to 3 days.

TAHINI MISO CAULIFLOWER

Another staple recipe in our house. Chuck everything on a tray, put it in the oven, and roast it all at once. So easy!

The dressing is one we make in bulk and keep in the fridge. So many fermented goodies in it, and it tastes totally amazing on everything.

SERVES 3

Prep time: 15–20 minutes
Cooking time: 20 minutes

1 cauliflower, cut into
    florets
1 red onion, cut into
    wedges
1 x 400g can chickpeas,
    drained and rinsed
1 tsp smoked paprika
1 tsp ground turmeric
pinch of sea salt
black pepper
oil
handful of fresh coriander,
    roughly chopped
3 tbsp tahini
3 tbsp black sesame
    seeds

Dressing
1 tbsp tahini
1 tsp apple cider vinegar
1 tsp miso paste
2–3 tbsp water

Preheat the oven to 200°C.

Place the cauliflower, onion and chickpeas on 2 baking trays. Sprinkle over the paprika, turmeric, salt, pepper and oil. Give everything a good toss.

Place in the oven for 10 minutes, then turn the oven to fan grill and cook for a further 10 minutes. Once cooked, remove from the oven.

To make the dressing, place all of the ingredients in a cup, and mix to combine.

Place the roasted cauliflower, onion and chickpeas into a large bowl, then drizzle over the dressing. Toss gently, until the dressing is evenly coating the cauliflower, onion and chickpeas. Add the chopped coriander, and give one final toss. Serve with some extra tahini and black sesame seeds.

Store any leftover salad in an airtight container in the fridge, where it will keep for up to 3–4 days.

POMEGRANATE MILLET KUMARA SALAD

Originating from the Middle East, pomegranate molasses is one of our favourite ingredients. The pomegranate juice is reduced down into a dark, thick liquid, which has an amazing mix of sweet, tangy and sour flavours. If anything needs a little something extra, this is the ingredient you need. This salad is a prime example, as it has such simple ingredients and flavours, but the pomegranate molasses ties everything together. For a fully plant-based meal we love serving this salad with hummus, or it is equally delicious with salmon or lamb.

SERVES 6

Prep time: 15 minutes
Cooking time: 25 minutes

2 kumara, cubed
oil
1 cup uncooked millet
2 cups water
1 bunch of kale, finely
    chopped
1 red onion, finely
    chopped
large handful of mint,
    roughly chopped

Dressing
1 tsp apple cider vinegar
2 tbsp water
2 tbsp extra virgin olive oil
2 tbsp pomegranate
    molasses
pinch of sea salt
juice of 1 lemon

Preheat the oven to 200°C.

Place the cubed kumara on a baking tray, and toss with the oil. Place in the oven, and bake for about 25 minutes, or until softened and golden.

Once cooked, remove from the oven and allow to cool slightly.

To make the dressing, place all of the ingredients in a cup, and mix to combine.

Place the millet and water in a pot, and bring to the boil. Reduce to a simmer, and cook for 10 minutes. Once cooked, remove from the heat. Allow to sit for 5–10 minutes, then fluff up the millet with a fork.

Place the cooked millet, kumara, kale, onion and mint in a big salad bowl, and pour over the dressing. Gently toss to combine.

Store any leftover salad in an airtight container in the fridge, where it will keep for up to 4–5 days.

FREEKEH, TOMATO, EGGPLANT + PRESERVED LEMON YOGHURT

Freekeh is a smoky cracked wheat, and is one of our favourites grains. This is one grain we use that isn't gluten-free, but if you want the recipe to be fully gluten-free, simply substitute the freekeh for quinoa, brown rice or millet. The smokiness from the freekeh goes so well with the roasted eggplant, cherry tomatoes and onion. Then the creamy, preserved lemon yoghurt dressing balances the pungent spices. This is delicious with salmon or lamb.

SERVES 4

Prep time: 15 minutes
Cooking time: 50 minutes

2 eggplants, cut into
　chunks
oil
pinch of sea salt
1 onion, thinly sliced
3 cloves of garlic,
　crushed and finely
　chopped
½ tsp smoked paprika
½ tsp ground cumin
2 cups (approx. 400g)
　cherry tomatoes
½ tbsp tomato paste
1½ cups water
1 cup freekeh

Yoghurt
100ml coconut yoghurt
¼ preserved lemon,
　finely chopped
small handful of fresh
　coriander, roughly
　chopped, plus extra
　to serve

Preheat the oven to 190°C.

Place the eggplant on a baking tray and drizzle with the oil and salt. Toss to combine.

Cook in the oven for 25–30 minutes, or until golden and completely softened, then remove from the oven.

Meanwhile heat some oil in a frying pan. Add the onion, and sauté to soften. Add the garlic, paprika, cumin and cherry tomatoes. Cook until the tomatoes have just softened, so you can crush them with the back of a fork.

Add the tomato paste and water, and make sure everything is combined well. Then stir through the freekeh. Bring it to the boil, then reduce to a simmer and cook for 12 minutes. Remove from the heat.

To make the yoghurt dressing, place all of the ingredients into a cup, and mix to combine.

To serve, divide the freekeh between bowls, and top with the roasted eggplant, yoghurt and some extra freshly chopped coriander.

Store any leftover salad in an airtight container in the fridge, where it will keep for up to 3 days.

TAHINI GREENS, FRIED GARLIC + CHILLI

You will convert all kale-haters with this recipe. The super-quick garlic- and chilli-infused oil gives the kale a delicious spicy kick. The tamari gives it a saltiness that is incredibly addictive. Top with crispy bits of garlic and chilli and tahini, and you will be in heaven.

SERVES 4

Prep time: 10 minutes
Cooking time: 10 minutes

2 tbsp olive oil
5 cloves of garlic, thinly
    sliced
1 red chilli, thinly sliced
a large bunch of kale
1 tbsp tamari
1 tbsp water
1–2 tbsp tahini

In a wok or large frying pan, heat the oil over a high heat. Once the oil is hot, add the garlic and chilli.

Fry off for 1–2 minutes, until the garlic is nice and golden. Remove the garlic and chilli from the wok or pan, leaving the frying oil, and set aside on paper towels.

Roughly rip up the kale, and add it to the wok or pan. Add the tamari and water.

Stir-fry the kale for 8 minutes, or until it starts to become browned and crispy on some parts.

Place the kale in a bowl, and drizzle with the tahini, and sprinkle over the fried garlic and chilli.

Store any leftovers in an airtight container in the fridge, where they will keep for up to 2 days.

NUTTY BLACK RICE, QUINOA + CARAMELISED ONIONS

This salad is a staple in our weekly meal plan. It's such a great one to make at the start of the week, because it lasts for a good 5 days, and develops in flavour as the days go on. Simply serve it with leftover roast veggies or a quick stir-fry. It is also a great one to feed a crowd.

The textures from the nuts, along with the tart, sweet taste of pomegranate molasses and cranberries, make this salad a stand-out.

SERVES 10–12

Prep time: 15–20 minutes
Cooking time: 35 minutes

1½ cups black rice
3 cups water
½ cup quinoa
1 cup water
1 tbsp oil
2 onions, thinly sliced
1 tsp ground cumin
½ cup flaked almonds, toasted
½ cup walnuts, toasted and roughly chopped
¼ cup pinenuts, toasted
large handful of flat-leaf parsley, roughly chopped
½ cup cranberries
zest and juice of 1 lemon
1 tbsp pomegranate molasses
1 tbsp extra virgin olive oil
2 cloves of garlic, crushed and finely chopped
handful of fresh rocket

Put the black rice in a pot, and add 3 cups water. Bring to the boil, and then reduce the heat to a simmer. Cook with the lid on for 20 minutes. Once cooked, allow to sit off the heat for 10–15 minutes.

In another pot, put the quinoa and add 1 cup of water. Bring to the boil, and then reduce the heat to a simmer. Cook for 5 minutes, then remove from the heat.

In a frying pan, heat the oil, then add the onion and cumin. Cook until nice and caramelised (about 10–15 minutes). Set aside.

Put the cooked rice and quinoa into a bowl. Add the onion, almonds, walnuts, pinenuts, parsley, cranberries, lemon zest and juice, pomegranate molasses, oil, garlic and rocket. Gently toss to combine everything together.

Store any leftover salad in an airtight container in the fridge, where it will keep for up to 5 days.

KALE AVOCADO TAHINI SALAD

Everyone wonders what they can do with kale. It can be bland on its own, so the key is massaging it in a mix of delicious flavours. Thanks to the lemon juice, the avocado won't go brown. If you don't have a lemon, add 1 tsp of apple cider vinegar instead.

We often make this as a green base for almost any salad. It is delicious with roast kumara and salmon.

SERVES 4–6

Prep time: 15 minutes

2 avocados, sliced
1 tbsp tahini
drizzle of sesame oil
juice of 1 lemon
pinch of chilli flakes
pinch of sea salt
1 bunch of kale, thinly
   sliced
½ cup toasted seeds
extra virgin olive oil, to
   drizzle

Put 1 avocado into a bowl, along with the tahini, sesame oil, lemon juice, chilli flakes and sea salt. Mash up the avocado with a fork, until everything is well-combined.

Add the kale, and massage it through the avocado mash.

Divide the kale salad between plates, and top with toasted seeds and the remaining avocado, and a drizzle of extra virgin olive oil.

Store any leftovers in an airtight container in the fridge, where they will keep for 1–2 days.

DUKKAH ROASTED CAULIFLOWER + AVOCADO DRESSING

This salad is one of our very first 2RS recipes. We had so many people disappointed that it wasn't in the first book, so here it is for you now. Roasted cauliflower with a creamy fresh avocado mint dressing and spicy crisp radish slices. The pastel colours scream summer, but it's great anytime you can get your hands on good avocados.

SERVES 4

Prep time: 15–20 minutes
Cooking time: 20 minutes

1 large head of cauliflower,
    cut into florets
2 x 400g cans chickpeas,
    drained and rinsed
oil
1 tbsp dukkah
pinch of sea salt
bunch of radishes,
    mandolined
large handful of fresh
    mint, roughly chopped
½ avocado, sliced

Dressing
½ avocado
½ cup coconut yoghurt
handful of fresh mint,
    roughly chopped
zest and juice of 1 lemon
pinch of sea salt
black pepper

Preheat the oven to 220°C.

Place the cauliflower and chickpeas onto 2 large baking trays, and drizzle with the oil. Top with the dukkah and salt, and toss to combine. Roast for 18–20 minutes, or until golden brown. Remove from the oven.

To make the dressing, place the avocado in a medium-sized bowl. Add the yoghurt, mint, lemon zest and juice, and salt and pepper. Using a hand-held blender or a food processor, blend until smooth and creamy.

Top the cauliflower and chickpeas with the radish, mint and remaining avocado. Drizzle with the creamy avocado dressing to serve.

Store any leftover salad in an airtight container in the fridge, where it will keep for up to 4 days.

CRISPY SMASHED POTATOES + GARLIC PESTO

All of the boys (and girls) will love these crispy potatoes. The trick is to boil them first, and then blast them on grill with lots of salt, resulting in a delicious salty, crispy outside. The garlic pesto is the cherry on top. Use any herbs you can get your hands on. Toasted pinenuts or cashews work great instead of walnuts.

If you're not familiar with nutritional yeast, they are flakes that are extremely high in vitamin B$_{12}$, and give you the cheesy flavour you would normally get from Parmesan cheese. You can get them at most health food stores and supermarkets.

SERVES 8

Prep time: 20 minutes
Cooking time: 45 minutes

8 medium-sized
   potatoes
oil
good pinch each of sea
   salt and black pepper
chopped herbs, to
   garnish

Pesto
1 packed cup fresh
   herbs (basil,
   coriander, rocket,
   mint, chives or
   parsley)
2 cloves of garlic,
   crushed and roughly
   chopped
¼ cup walnuts, toasted
juice of ½ lemon
1½ tbsp nutritional
   yeast
2–3 tbsp extra virgin
   olive oil
good pinch of sea salt
black pepper

Preheat the oven to 200°C. Line a baking tray with baking paper, and set aside.

Put the rinsed potatoes into a large pot, and cover with water until just submerged. Bring to the boil over a high heat. Reduce to a medium–high heat to achieve a low boil. Cook uncovered for 15–20 minutes, or until tender and a knife easily slides in and out.

In the meantime, prepare the pesto by placing all of the ingredients into a food processor, and blend to combine. Transfer to a small serving dish and set aside.

When the potatoes are soft and tender, place them on the baking tray, and smash them down with the bottom of a clean saucepan. Cut any larger potatoes in half and then smash them, so they are still bite-size.

Drizzle the potatoes with the oil, and season with the salt and pepper. Roast for 20–25 minutes, or until crispy and golden brown.

To serve, spoon the pesto over the potatoes. Garnish with additional chopped herbs.

Store any leftover potatoes in an airtight container in the fridge, where they will keep for up to 3 days.

KALE, GRILLED BROCCOLI + EDAMAME SALAD

We make this salad most weeks, as it's so quick and easy to whip together when you can't be bothered cooking or have minimal time. The miso and extra virgin olive oil give the kale an addictive salty, umami flavour. The drizzle of sesame oil and tahini is amazing, too. We often serve it with stir-fried broccoli and zucchini, and half an avocado, to make it a complete meal. It's also amazing with salmon.

SERVES 6–8

Prep time: 10–15 minutes
Cooking time: 10 minutes

8 stalks kale, leaves removed and
    stalks discarded
2 tbsp extra virgin olive oil
1 tbsp white wine vinegar
1 heaped tsp miso paste
pinch of sea salt
1 cup edamame beans, blanched in
    boiling water, then drained
¼ cup pumpkin seeds, toasted
oil
pinch of sea salt
½ head of broccoli, cut into florets

tahini
sesame oil

Put the kale leaves into a bowl, along with olive oil, vinegar, miso and sea salt. Massage until the kale softens. Add the edamame beans and pumpkin seeds. Toss to combine.

Heat a frying pan, add some oil and salt, and cook the broccoli until lightly charred.

To serve, spread the kale mix out onto a platter, top with grilled broccoli, and drizzle over the tahini and sesame oil.

Store any leftover salad in an airtight container in the fridge, where it will keep for up to 3 days.

STUFFED KUMARA

Soft and sweet baked kumara stuffed with all the goodies — like mushrooms, pesto, creamy tahini, smooth avocado and crunchy nuts and seeds. All of these flavours and textures make this a favourite go-to when we are after a filling plant-based meal. If we need a vegetable boost, we love to add other veggies like broccoli and zucchini.

If we are super-organised we will pre-cook some kumara for dinners throughout the week. Then all we have to do is stir-fry up some veggies we have in the fridge and add lots of delicious toppings. Simple, yet delicious.

SERVES 2

Prep time: 20 minutes
Cooking time: 1 hour

2 kumara (purple or
    orange)
oil
¼ head of broccoli, cut
    into florets
1 zucchini, sliced thinly
    lengthways
2 spring onions, sliced

** Feel free to change up
which vegetables you use,
depending on the season
and what's available.
It's great with cherry
tomatoes, mushrooms,
cauliflower, etc.*

couple of handfuls
    of spinach
2 tbsp tahini
2 tbsp pesto
½–1 avocado, cut into
    slices
¼ cup toasted seeds
    or nuts

Preheat the oven to 200°C.

Pierce some holes in the kumara, place on a baking tray, and bake for 45–50 minutes. Take out of the oven, and allow to cool slightly.

Put the oil into a frying pan, and sauté the broccoli, zucchini and spring onions (and any other vegetables of your choice) for about 5–10 minutes.

Cut the cooked kumara down the middle lengthways with a knife, and slightly pull it apart with your hands. Then stuff the kumara with the cooked broccoli, zucchini and spring onion. Then top with spinach, tahini, pesto, avocado and toasted seeds or nuts.

Other delicious things to stuff the kumara with include: hummus, black beans, salsa, crispy chickpeas, chilli flakes, roasted eggplant, pea smash.

Store any leftover (unstuffed) kumara in an airtight container in the fridge, where it will keep for up to 3 days. Enjoy cold, or reheat.

ROASTED SUMAC PUMPKIN, WALNUTS + COCONUT HERB TAHINI DRESSING

We have turned a good old roast pumpkin salad into something with a bit of a wow factor, with the herb tahini dressing, earthy walnuts and pops of pomegranate seeds. This can all be made in advance, as the dressing will keep in the fridge for up to 1 week. Serve alongside a green salad, and roast lamb, chicken or salmon, or hummus and avocado for a fully plant-based meal.

SERVES 8–10

Prep time: 20–25 minutes
Cooking time: 30 minutes

½ butternut pumpkin, cut
   into chunks
1 red onion, sliced
1½ tbsp ground sumac
   powder
pinch of sea salt
oil
handful of fresh rocket
¾ cup walnuts, roasted
   and roughly chopped
seeds of ½ pomegranate
4 tbsp dukkah

Dressing
¼ cup tahini
¼ cup coconut yoghurt
¼ cup extra virgin olive oil
1 cup fresh herbs, roughly
   chopped (mint, coriander,
   rocket, parsley)
3 tbsp water
2 cloves of garlic, crushed
   and finely chopped
1 tsp ground sumac
   powder
juice of 1 lemon
pinch of sea salt
black pepper

Preheat the oven to 200°C.

Put the pumpkin and onion on 2 baking trays, sprinkle over the sumac and sea salt, and drizzle the oil. Toss to coat the pumpkin and onion evenly.

Place the baking trays in the oven for 20 minutes on fan bake, then turn the oven onto its grill function and grill for 10 minutes.

Meanwhile make the tahini dressing. Put all of the ingredients into a blender, and blitz until a smooth, creamy dressing is formed. Pour into a bowl and set aside.

To plate the salad, get a flat, round salad plate. Put down a layer of rocket, followed by half of the roasted pumpkin, dressing, walnuts and pomegranate seeds, then sprinkle with dukkah. Repeat this process for another layer.

Store any leftovers in an airtight container in the fridge, where they will keep for up to 3–4 days. If there is any leftover dressing, store it in a glass jar or container in the fridge, where it will keep for up to 1 week.

ROSEMARY ROASTED VEGETABLES + SUMAC CAPER SALSA

This is a great way to spice up your normal roast veggie salad. Salsas are a lifesaver when you have little time but need to make something with a bit of wow to it. This salsa is particularly delicious with the salty bombs of capers, the nutty pinenuts and the tart sumac. These vegetables are our favourite winter mix, but feel free to change it up with some summer produce. Delicious served with lamb.

SERVES 6–8

Prep time: 20–25 minutes
Cooking time: 30 minutes

2 parsnips, cut into sticks
2 red onions, sliced
3 kumara, cut into sticks
1 leek, sliced
1 bulb of garlic, cloves
   individually separated
4 sprigs of rosemary, leaves
   removed and stalks
   discarded
zest of 1 lemon
2 tbsp oil
pinch of sea salt
black pepper
250g punnet cherry tomatoes

Salsa
handful of flat-leaf parsley,
   roughly chopped
1 tbsp red wine vinegar
4 tbsp capers
2 tbsp pinenuts, toasted (or any
   nut or seed of your choice)
1 tsp ground sumac powder
1 tsp wholegrain or Dijon
   mustard
black pepper

Preheat the oven to 190°C.

Evenly divide the cut vegetables between 2 baking trays. Add the garlic cloves, rosemary leaves, lemon zest, oil, salt and pepper. Toss to combine.

Place in the oven. After 20 minutes, turn the oven onto its grill function, divide the cherry tomatoes between the 2 trays, and grill for a further 10 minutes. Remove from the oven.

To make the salsa, place all of the ingredients in a bowl, and gently mix to combine.

Divide the salsa between the 2 trays, and toss to combine.

Serve either straight from the trays, or on a big platter. Delicious served with dollops of yoghurt or crumbled feta.

Store any leftover salad in an airtight container in the fridge, where it will keep for up to 4 days.

MISO PUMPKIN SOUP

Pumpkin soup is one of our favourites in winter, and this recipe is just the best. The coconut cream makes it so deliciously creamy, and the miso takes it to the next level with an amazing salty, umami undertone.

So easy to make: we love to freeze half of the batch in portion sizes, so we have them ready as easy pull-out dinners on busy weeks.

SERVES 6

Prep time: 15 minutes
Cooking time: 40 minutes

½ large pumpkin
oil
1 large brown onion, diced
1 tbsp curry powder
1 L water
1 x 400ml can coconut
  cream
3 tbsp miso paste
pinch of salt
black pepper

Preheat the oven to 200°C.

De-seed the pumpkin, and cut it into small chunks, leaving the skin on.

Place the pumpkin on a baking tray, drizzle with some oil, and toss to combine. Roast in the oven for 20–25 minutes, or until soft and slightly charred.

Once the pumpkin is cooked, heat a large soup pot over a medium heat. Add a good drizzle of oil, along with the onion. Sauté until it becomes translucent, about 5–8 minutes. Add the curry powder, and cook off for 1 minute.

Add the water, roasted pumpkin and coconut cream, stir, and bring to the boil. Once the soup is at a boil, take it off the heat and add the miso paste.

Using a stick blender, blend the soup until it is silky smooth. Add salt and pepper to taste.

This soup will keep in the fridge for up to 2 weeks, or in the freezer for up to 3 months.

CREAMY MUSHROOM GARLIC SOUP + HERB OIL

Mushrooms make a lovely base for this soup. Their earthy flavour is complemented so well with the garlic and bay leaves. It is bulked up with the creamy coconut milk and salty fermented miso. The herb oil adds a vibrant, fresh green colour. If you don't want to make the oil, fresh chopped herbs and a drizzle of olive oil or hemp oil will work just as well.

SERVES 4

Prep time: 20–25 minutes
Cooking time: 20 minutes

oil
1 brown onion, diced
5 cloves of garlic, crushed
    and roughly chopped
2 bay leaves
400g Portobello
    mushrooms, sliced
1 x 400ml can of coconut
    milk
800ml water
2 tbsp miso paste
pinch of sea salt
black pepper

Herb oil
2 cups fresh herbs (parsley,
    mint, rocket, coriander),
    roughly chopped
⅓ cup extra virgin olive oil
juice of ½ lemon
pinch of sea salt
black pepper

Heat a large soup pot over a medium heat, then add the oil and diced onion. Sauté until the onion becomes translucent. Just before this happens, add the garlic and bay leaves. Cook for another 5 minutes.

Add the mushrooms, and fry off for a further 5–10 minutes, or until the mushrooms look half-cooked.

Add the coconut milk, and then fill up the empty coconut milk can twice with water, and pour into the pot. Bring to the boil, and simmer for 5 minutes.

Take the soup off the heat and remove the bay leaves. Add the miso. Blend the soup until smooth with a stick blender or blender. Season to taste.

To make the herb oil, blend all of the ingredients in a jug with a stick blender, until smooth.

Serve the soup with a dollop of the herb oil and garlic-rubbed sourdough.

This soup will keep in the fridge for up to 2 weeks, or in the freezer for up to 3 months. We freeze it in portions so it's super-easy to pull out when we have nothing at hand for lunch or dinner.

GREEN SPINACH + TAHINI SOUP

This soup is packed full of so many greens and fermented goodies. The addition of tahini is what we use instead of cream to make the soup nice and creamy. (This is a great tip for any recipe if you are dairy-free.) Miso paste is fermented soy beans. In all of our soups we use it as a stock base instead of processed stocks from the supermarket. However, always remember to add the miso once you have finished the cooking process; if it is heated for a long time, all of the beneficial probiotics will denature.

SERVES 4

Prep time: 20–25 minutes
Cooking time: 20 minutes

2 tbsp oil
1 brown onion, diced
2 stalks of celery, diced
2 cloves of garlic, crushed
    and roughly chopped
5–6 cups white
    mushrooms, sliced
1½ tbsp tamari
pinch of sea salt
black pepper
6 cups water
handful of kale, roughly
    chopped
150–200g baby spinach
1½ cups edamame beans
    or peas
2–4 tbsp miso paste
2 tbsp tahini

Put the oil in a pot, and add the diced onion. Sauté for a few minutes, then add the celery, garlic, mushrooms, tamari, salt and pepper. Cook until softened.

Add the water and bring to a simmer.

Once simmering, add the kale, baby spinach and edamame beans or peas. Once the greens have wilted, remove from the heat.

Add the miso paste and tahini. Blitz the soup until smooth, using a stick blender or blender.

Serve hot, topped with Creamy Tahini Chickpeas (page 136).

This soup will keep in the fridge for up to 2 weeks, or in the freezer for up to 3 months. We freeze it in portions so it's super-easy to pull out when we have nothing at hand for lunch or dinner.

CREAMY TAHINI CHICKPEAS

If, like us, you do not tolerate gluten (aka bread) very well, it's quite hard in winter when soup season is in full swing. Soup without bread isn't quite the same. These tahini chickpeas are a great substitute for the missing bread. Coated in creamy tahini and fresh, fragrant herbs, they are perfect to make a soup more substantial and add great texture. Use these to bulk up salads in the warmer months as well!

SERVES 4–6

Prep time: 10 minutes

2 x 400g can chickpeas,
    drained and rinsed
3 tbsp tahini
1 tbsp extra virgin oil
juice of 1 lemon
small handful of fresh
    herbs, roughly chopped
2 good pinches of sea salt
black pepper

Mix all of the ingredients together in a bowl, until the chickpeas are well-coated.

MISO MUSHROOM RICE

When we did this in an online workshop, it was an absolute hit, so we had to put it in cookbook #2!

This is like a fried rice, with all of the pungent Asian flavours, like the garlic, ginger, tamari and sesame oil. The addition of miso adds a delicious depth of salty, umami flavour to the rice.

Mushrooms are a great veggie for this dish, because they absorb all of the beautiful flavours. However, feel free to add others veggies, such as zucchini or broccoli.

SERVES 2

Prep time: 20–25 minutes
Cooking time: 50 minutes (includes cooking time for brown rice)

1 cup brown rice
2 cups water
1 tbsp oil
1 red onion, thinly sliced
1 clove of garlic, crushed and
    finely chopped
1 tbsp fresh ginger, grated
4 cups mixed mushrooms,
    sliced (we used white button
    and Portobello)
6 tbsp coconut cream
2 tbsp tamari
1 tsp sesame oil
zest of 1 lemon
pinch of chilli flakes
pinch of sea salt
black pepper
½ cup edamame beans,
    blanched in boiling water,
    then drained
1 tbsp miso, mixed with
    2 tbsp water
4 tbsp sesame seeds, toasted
3 spring onions, thinly sliced
handful of coriander, roughly
    chopped

Cook the rice, according to the packet instructions.

Meanwhile, heat the oil in a medium-sized frying pan. Add the onion, and sauté until softened and slightly browned (about 5 minutes). Add the garlic and ginger, and continue to sauté for another couple of minutes.

Add the mushrooms and 3 tablespoons of the coconut cream, and sauté until mushrooms have softened.

Then add the cooked brown rice, the remaining 3 tablespoons of the coconut cream, the tamari, sesame oil, lemon zest, chilli flakes, and salt and pepper. Mix until well-combined. Simmer for 5–10 minutes.

Remove the pan from the heat, and stir through edamame beans, miso, sesame seeds and spring onion. Top with fresh coriander. This is great served warm or cold.

Store any leftovers in an airtight container in the fridge, where they will keep for up to 3–4 days.

ROASTED EGGPLANT + CHICKPEA CURRY

This curry is so ridiculously easy to make, and is packed with so much flavour thanks to all of the pungent spices.

We always say in our workshops that everyone needs to utilise spices more instead of store-bought sauces. Unprocessed spices have so much more flavour and nutrients! Making curries is a great example of this. The soft eggplant absorbs all of the amazing Indian spices, and the chickpeas add a lovey bite. We encourage you to make this and realise just how easy it is to make your own curry from scratch. This is amazing served with some brown rice, seasonal greens, extra coriander and a dollop of coconut yoghurt.

SERVES 3–4

Prep time: 20–25 minutes
Cooking time: 35 minutes

2 medium eggplants, cut
  into cubes
oil
pinch of sea salt
black pepper
1 tsp cumin seeds
pinch of chilli flakes
4 cloves of garlic, crushed
  and finely chopped
1 tbsp fresh grated ginger
1 onion, thinly sliced
1 tbsp curry powder
1 tbsp ground garam
  masala
1 tsp ground turmeric
1 tsp coconut sugar
1 x 400g can chopped
  tomatoes
1 x 400g can chickpeas,
  drained and rinsed
3 tbsp coconut yoghurt
handful of fresh coriander,
  roughly chopped

Preheat the oven to 200°C.

Place the eggplant on the baking tray and drizzle with the oil and sea salt and pepper. Cook in the oven for 25 minutes.

While the eggplant is cooking, put some more oil into a large frying pan or pot, and add the cumin seeds, chilli, garlic, ginger and onion. Cook over a medium heat, until the onion softens and becomes slightly golden brown.

Add the curry powder, garam masala, turmeric and coconut sugar. Give it a good mix, and continue to cook for another 2–3 minutes.

Add the chopped tomatoes and chickpeas, and let it simmer for about 5 minutes. Lastly stir through the cooked eggplant, and add the coconut yoghurt and coriander.

Store any leftovers in an airtight container in the fridge, where they will keep for up to 3–4 days. Or you can freeze into portions, which will keep for up to 1 month.

MISO MUSHROOM TOMATO PASTA

Everyone has a soft spot for pasta. We posted this on our blog, and it blew up. Garlic, rosemary, tomatoes, capers, miso and mushrooms. Oh my gosh, all the best things mixed into comforting swirls of pasta … And this is delicious sprinkled with nutritional yeast.

We normally make this on a night when we arrive home after a big day at work and realise we have nothing in the fridge, and all we need is a big comfort-food belly-hug.

SERVES 4

Prep time: 15–20 minutes
Cooking time: 35 minutes

1 x 250–300g packet of pasta (we love sorghum, chickpea and red lentil)
oil
1 onion, finely chopped
5 cloves of garlic, crushed and finely chopped
1 sprig of rosemary, finely chopped
pinch of sea salt
450g mushrooms, sliced
1 x 400g can cherry tomatoes
handful of fresh cherry tomatoes (or use another tin of tomatoes)
5 heaped tsp tomato purée
1 tsp smoked paprika
150–200g spinach
3 tbsp miso paste
pinch of chilli flakes
1 tsp apple cider vinegar
1 tbsp capers
juice of ½ lemon
pinch of sea salt
black pepper

Cook the pasta according to the packet instructions. Drain and set aside.

Heat a good glug of olive oil in a wok or a large frying pan, then add the onion, garlic, rosemary and salt. Cook until the onion softens.

Add the mushrooms, and cook for 10 minutes, or until the mushrooms become soft. Then add the tomatoes, tomato purée and paprika. Continue to cook for a further 5 minutes. Remove from the heat.

Stir in the spinach, miso, chilli flakes, apple cider vinegar, capers, lemon juice, and salt and pepper to taste. Allow the spinach to wilt.

To serve, divide between bowls.

Store any leftovers in an airtight container in the fridge, where they will keep for up to 3–4 days.

ROASTED STUFFED EGGPLANT

We have a huge love for eggplant. This is one of our most frequently made recipes. They keep for 5 days in the fridge, so we make a batch and keep them for easy, effortless work lunches or quick dinners. The soft baked eggplant flesh is mixed through tomatoes, onion, garlic, brown rice and nutritional yeast — totally delicious. To make it a fully plant-based meal we love serving it with avocado, tamari stir-fried broccoli, fresh greens and a good sprinkle of nutritional yeast. It is equally delicious as a side to slow-cooked lamb.

SERVES 2

Prep time: 15 minutes
Cooking time:
55–60 minutes

½ cup brown rice
1 cup water
2 eggplants
oil
2 tsp sea salt
1 onion, chopped
1 clove of garlic,
   crushed and finely
   chopped
½ tsp ground cumin
2 tbsp tomato paste
½ x 400g can crushed
   tomatoes
black pepper
¼ cup nutritional yeast
2–3 tbsp pinenuts

Preheat the oven to 200°C.

Cook the brown rice, according to the packet instructions.

Meanwhile, cut the eggplants in half lengthways, leaving the stems intact. Place them cut side up on a baking tray. Drizzle with oil and season with salt. Bake for 30 minutes, until soft and lightly browned.

While the eggplant is baking, make the tomato sauce. Heat some oil in a frying pan on a medium heat, and cook the onion and garlic until soft, 3–4 minutes. Add the cumin, tomato paste and crushed tomatoes. Simmer for 8–10 minutes, stirring frequently, until a thick chutney-like consistency. Season to taste with salt and pepper.

When the eggplant has finished baking, remove it from the oven and scoop out the soft flesh with a spoon, being careful not to tear the skin. Mix the soft eggplant flesh into the tomato sauce. Lightly mix the tomato eggplant sauce with the cooked rice and nutritional yeast. Fill the eggplant halves with the mixture, dividing equally.

Sprinkle with pinenuts. Return to the oven for another 5–10 minutes, or until crispy and golden on top.

Store any leftovers in an airtight container in the fridge, where they will keep for up to 5 days.

ALFREDO SAUCE

Sunflower seeds are a life hack to cheaper plant-based cream sauces (sweet or savoury). Most recipes use cashews as the base, but they can be really expensive and heavy on the gut. Sunflower seeds are much lighter, but still give you the same decadent creamy end result.

This sauce freezes really well, so we freeze it in portions and take them out as we need them.

MAKES APPROX. 2 CUPS

Prep time: 15 minutes

1 cup sunflower seeds,
    softened in boiling water
    for 5–10 minutes, then
    drained and rinsed
½ cup water
pinch of sea salt
1 clove of garlic, crushed and
    roughly chopped
½ shallot, roughly chopped
¼ tsp nutritional yeast
black pepper

Place all of the ingredients into a blender, and blend until creamy and smooth.

Store any leftovers in an airtight container or glass jar in the fridge, where it will keep for up to 7 days. Alternatively, freeze for up to 1 month.

CREAMY MUSHROOM ALFREDO PASTA

Creamy Alfredo Sauce mixed through thyme- and garlic-infused mushrooms and pasta. Oh my goodness, this pasta is to die for. It is so easy to put together if you already have your Alfredo Sauce frozen in portions. All you need to do is pull it out of the freezer in the morning before work, and when you get home simply cook the pasta and mushrooms. Done.

SERVES 2

Prep time: 10–15 minutes
Cooking time: 15–20 minutes

approx. 150g pasta
   (sorghum, chickpea and
   red lentil)
oil
1 white onion, diced
2 cloves of garlic, crushed
   and finely chopped
2 heaped cups chopped
   mushrooms, mix of
   Portobello and white
2 sprigs of fresh thyme or
   rosemary
pinch of sea salt
black pepper
½ cup Alfredo Sauce
   (page 147)
handful of fresh parsley,
   finely chopped

Cook the pasta, according to the packet instructions, and set aside.

Heat the oil in a frying pan, then add the diced onion and garlic. Sauté for a couple of minutes to soften. Then add the mushrooms, herbs, and salt and pepper.

Once the mushrooms are cooked, mix through the Alfredo Sauce, and cook for a further 2–3 minutes to warm up the sauce. Take off the heat and stir through the pasta and fresh parsley.

Store any leftovers in an airtight container in the fridge, where they will keep for up to 3 days.

TEMPEH PATTIES

Tempeh is like tofu, but it is fermented and the beans are roughly chopped, so it has a lot more texture.

Here we have crumbled it and mixed it through a delicious mix of sundried tomatoes, onion, garlic, sage, thyme and smoked paprika. These are a great way to bulk up a plant-based meal, or they make great burger patties! Give them a go for your weekly meal prep.

MAKES 4

Prep time: 20 minutes
Cooking time: 30–40 minutes

250g tempeh
1 onion, finely chopped
1 tbsp olive oil
2 cloves of garlic, crushed
   and finely chopped
2 tbsp tamari
1 tbsp chopped sage
1 tbsp chopped thyme
1½ tbsp brown rice flour
1 tsp smoked paprika
½ tsp fennel seeds
½ cup sundried tomatoes,
   roughly chopped
pinch of salt
black pepper
brown rice flour, for coating

Boil the tempeh for 20 minutes on a medium–high heat.

Meanwhile cook the onion in a frying pan with the olive oil for 3–4 minutes, then add the crushed garlic and continue to cook for an extra 1 minute. Allow to cool.

Put everything, except for the tempeh, into a food processor, and process until well-combined.

Break up the tempeh into rough chunks, and add to the food processor. Pulse until everything is well-combined.

Shape the mixture into patties, and then lightly coat with flour.

Heat a frying pan with oil, and cook the patties for 4–5 minutes on each side, or until cooked.

Store any leftovers in an airtight container in the fridge, where they will keep for up to 5 days. Or freeze for up to 1 month.

AVOCADO PESTO PASTA BAKE

This pasta bake is seriously to die for. It is so easy, and uses minimal, cheap ingredients. In the pesto, the avocado creates a delicious creaminess, and the nutritional yeast gives a cheesy flavour. The two marry together to mimic a traditional cheesy cream sauce, but instead with nutrient-dense ingredients.

Pop it in the oven for 15 minutes, and the result is punchy pops of tomato bombs and a crisp, crunchy top of creamy, cheesy, pesto pasta.

SERVES 2

Prep time: 20 minutes
Cooking time: 25 minutes (includes time for cooking pasta)

1 x 250–300g packet of pasta (sorghum, chickpea and red lentil)
1 punnet (approx. 180g) cherry tomatoes
½ cup sundried tomatoes
nutritional yeast, to sprinkle

Pesto
1 ripe avocado, skin and stone removed
¼ cup walnuts or pinenuts, toasted
2 cloves of garlic, crushed and finely chopped
juice of 1 lemon
¼ cup nutritional yeast
¼ cup extra virgin olive oil
pinch of salt
black pepper

Preheat the oven to 200°C.

Cook the pasta, according to the packet instructions. Once cooked, place the pasta in a large bowl and set aside.

To make the pesto, place all of the ingredients into a bowl. Using a stick blender, blitz everything together, until smooth and creamy. Add the pesto to the bowl of cooked pasta, and mix to evenly coat the pasta.

Add the cherry tomatoes and sundried tomatoes, and mix everything together.

Pour the pasta mix into an ovenproof dish. Sprinkle with extra nutritional yeast, and place in the oven to cook for 15 minutes. Serve hot or cold, with a side of stir-fried greens.

Store any leftovers in an airtight container in the fridge, where they will keep for up to 4 days.

DESSERTS

We are huge sweet-tooths and love a good dessert. The best thing about these recipes is they are made with only whole, unprocessed raw ingredients. We know how expensive and time-consuming raw desserts can be to make, which is why all of the following desserts are purposely made with the most cost-effective ingredients and ones you will already be familiar with and have at home. If they cannot be eaten right there and then, they all have minimal setting times of 1–3 hours.

If you are gluten-free and/or eat dairy, see page 9.

MANGO SOFT SERVE

We have a big soft spot for frozen mango. It makes the perfect instant ice cream, and has such an amazing colour.

This soft serve is filled with so many fermented goodies. The coconut yoghurt makes it incredibly creamy, and the apple cider vinegar gives it an addictive tang. Make this for breakfast or dessert; we love serving it with a sprinkle of granola to give it a little crunch.

SERVES 2–4

Prep time: 10 minutes

500g frozen mango
1 cup coconut yoghurt
2 tbsp 100% pure maple
   syrup
2 tsp apple cider vinegar
1 tsp vanilla bean paste or
   extract

Place all ingredients into a blender or food processor, and blend until smooth.

Divide between bowls and eat immediately.

Alternatively, store it in a snap-lock container or a metal tin in the freezer for up to 1 month, taking it out 15 minutes before eating.

STRAWBERRIES WITH HONEY- + THYME-SCENTED YOGHURT

Roasting strawberries gives them the most amazing intense depth of flavour, and it is so easy to do.

Served alongside a beautiful, fragrant honey- and thyme-infused yoghurt, this is the perfect melt-in-your-mouth summer dessert. Leftover yoghurt and strawberries are great on top of granola for breakfast.

SERVES 4

Prep time: 15 minutes
Cooking time: 10 minutes

1 punnet strawberries
1 tsp vanilla bean paste
    or extract

Scented yoghurt
1 tsp coconut oil
2 tbsp honey
3 tbsp fresh thyme
    leaves (save 1 tbsp for
    garnishing)
¾ cup coconut yoghurt

Preheat the oven to 200°C.

Cut the strawberries in half and place on a baking tray. Add the vanilla, and give it a good mix. Place in the oven for 10 minutes.

While the strawberries cook, make the yoghurt. Heat up a pan over a medium heat, then put in the coconut oil, honey and 2 tablespoons of the thyme. Let the mixture bubble for about 20 seconds. Turn the mixture onto a low heat, and let it infuse with the thyme for 5 minutes, stirring every now and then.

Put the coconut yoghurt into a small bowl. Pour three-quarters of the infused honey mixture into the yoghurt, and mix until well-combined. Set aside. Leave the remaining quarter of infused honey on a very low heat.

When the roasted strawberries are ready, take them out of the oven, and let them cool for 5–10 minutes.

Spread the infused yoghurt on a flat plate, and place the roasted strawberries on top. Drizzle with the remaining honey and fresh thyme leaves. Eat immediately.

POMEGRANATE AND ORANGE MARINATED STRAWBERRIES + ICE CREAM

The perfect light summer dessert. Sweet, ripe strawberries, zesty orange, tangy pomegranate molasses, silky maple syrup and delicate vanilla. If strawberries aren't in season, in winter we love marinating pears and roasting them.

Serve with vanilla bean ice cream and our Sweet and Salty Crunch (page 163).

SERVES 4

Prep time: 10 minutes
Marinating time:
20–30 minutes

1 punnet strawberries,
   sliced
zest and juice of 1 orange
1 tsp pomegranate
   molasses
2 tsp 100% pure maple
   syrup
½ tsp vanilla bean paste
   or extract
vanilla bean ice cream

Place the sliced strawberries in a medium-sized bowl. Add the remaining ingredients, except the ice cream, and mix until well-combined. Leave to marinate for 20–30 minutes, so the fruit can be infused with the syrup flavours. The longer you leave them marinating, the softer the strawberries will become.

Once marinated, place a scoop of ice cream into each bowl, and top with the marinated strawberries and a sprinkle of Sweet and Salty Crunch (page 163).

SWEET AND SALTY CRUNCH

We make this all the time when we are entertaining. It takes 2 minutes to make, and it adds such a wow factor to any dessert. Use it as a topping on ice cream for a bit of crunch. Mix it through melted chocolate to make a bark, or serve it with roasted stone fruit in summer.

SERVES 4–6

Prep time: 5 minutes

1 cup nuts, roasted and
    roughly chopped (whole
    or slivered almonds, Brazil
    nuts, cashews, walnuts)
2 tbsp sweetener (100% pure
    maple syrup or honey)
pinch of sea salt

In a small bowl, combine the nuts with the sweetener and salt. Adjust the seasoning as you like. Mix until well-combined and the nuts are nicely coated in sweetener. Serve immediately.

AVOCADO LIME MOUSSE CAKE

Avocado makes the perfect filling for cheesecakes. It creates a beautiful light, creamy consistency compared to traditional raw cheesecakes, which are filled with nuts, making them quite heavy.

The freshness from the lime makes this the perfect palate cleanser to finish any meal.

SERVES 8

Prep time: 25 minutes
Setting time: 2–3 hours

Base
½ cup sunflower seeds
1 cup desiccated coconut
½ cup dates, softened
   in boiling water for
   5–10 minutes, then
   drained
1 tbsp ground ginger
pinch of sea salt

Mousse
¾ cup cashews, softened
   in boiling water, then
   drained
1 avocado
1 cup coconut milk
⅓ cup coconut oil, melted
⅓ cup 100% pure maple
   syrup
zest and juice of 5 limes
pinch of sea salt

To make the base, place the sunflower seeds and coconut into a blender or food processor, and blend into a fine flour. Add the remaining base ingredients, and blend until you have a cookie-dough consistency.

Line a cake tin with beeswax wrap or cling film. Evenly press the base into the tin, and flatten it with the back of a spoon. Set the base aside.

For the mousse, place all of the ingredients in the blender, and blend until super-smooth and creamy.

Pour the mousse over the base, and bang the tin a few times on your bench top to remove any air bubbles, so you get a smooth finish. Place in the freezer to set, for 2–3 hours, then serve.

If you are pre-preparing it, slice the cake into pieces, and store in an airtight container in the freezer for up to 2 months. When you are wanting to eat it, allow about 10–15 minutes for it to thaw.

CHOCOLATE WALNUT FUDGE

This fudge will literally melt in your mouth. It is so silky smooth, and spiked with crunchy chunks of earthy walnuts to give some texture. It is a great dessert to have in the freezer for when unexpected guests arrive, or when you need to satisfy that sweet tooth.

MAKES 10

Prep time: 15 minutes
Cooking time: 15 minutes
Setting time: 1 hour

1 cup walnuts, toasted
    and roughly chopped
1 tbsp + 1 tsp honey
flesh of 1 avocado
10 dried figs, softened in
    boiling water for 5–10
    minutes, then drained
1 tsp vanilla bean paste or
    extract
2 tbsp coconut oil, melted
3 tbsp cacao powder
½ tsp ground ginger
½ tsp ground cinnamon
pinch of sea salt

Line a loaf tin with baking paper. Set aside.

Put the walnuts in a pan over a medium heat. Add 1 tablespoon of honey, allow to melt, and stir to evenly coat the walnuts in honey. Cook for around 5 minutes, or until the nuts start to go a nice golden brown. Remove from the heat.

Into a blender or food processor, place the avocado, figs, the other teaspoon of honey, vanilla, coconut oil, cacao, ginger, cinnamon and salt. Blend until a smooth mixture is formed.

Add the walnuts to the chocolate mixture. Mix until everything is well-combined.

Line a loaf tin with beeswax wraps or cling film. Pour the mixture into the lined tin and evenly press down, using the back of a spoon. Place in the freezer for 1 hour, to set. Remove, and cut into pieces.

Store any leftover fudge in an airtight container in the fridge, where it will keep for up to 1–2 weeks, or in the freezer, where it will keep for up to 2 months.

PEANUT CHOCOLATE LAYER BARS

We eat sandwiches all the time, so why not have one for dessert? Salted honey coconut and crunchy peanut butter layers sandwiched between two thick slabs of chocolate — need we say more? Eat these as they are, or cut them into chunks to have with ice cream.

MAKES 8

Prep time: 25 minutes
Setting time: 40 minutes

200g dark chocolate,
    roughly chopped
1 cup shredded
    coconut
¼ cup roasted peanuts,
    roughly chopped
¼ cup runny honey
1 tbsp coconut oil,
    melted
½ tsp sea salt
2 tbsp tahini
4 tbsp peanut butter
    (we used smooth)

Line a loaf tin with a beeswax wrap or cling film. Set aside.

Melt the chocolate using a double boiler.

While the chocolate is melting, make the coconut filling. Place the coconut, peanuts, honey, coconut oil and salt in a medium-sized bowl. Mix together, until it all sticks together and is well-combined.

When the chocolate is melted, add the tahini. Whisk until everything is well-combined. Pour half of the chocolate into the lined loaf tin. Place in the freezer for 5–10 minutes to set.

Once the chocolate is set, spread 2 tbsp of peanut butter over the chocolate. Now add the coconut mixture, pressing it down firmly with the back of a spoon until it is evenly spread out.

Spread another 2 tbsp of peanut butter evenly over the coconut mixture, followed by the remaining chocolate. Place in the freezer for 20–30 minutes to set.

Once the bar is set, cut it into slices.

Store in an airtight container in the freezer, where it will keep for up to 3 months.

PERKY NANA BROWNIE BARS

Cadbury Perky Nana Bars were a childhood favourite of ours. If you were also a fan, these will bring back some nostalgic feelings and flavours. Bite into the chocolate ganache to reveal the sweet, caramelised yellow banana filling. We just know you are going to love these!

MAKES 10

Prep time: 30 minutes
Cooking time: 20 minutes
Setting time: 3–4 hours

Brownie
1 cup walnuts or rolled oats
1 cup desiccated coconut
½ cup dates, softened
   in boiling water for
   5–10 minutes, then drained
½ cup cacao powder
pinch of sea salt

Banana ice cream
4 ripe bananas
¾ cup coconut milk
⅓ cup coconut oil, melted
½ cup cashews, softened
   in boiling water for
   5–10 minutes, then drained
½ cup dates, softened
   in boiling water for
   5–10 minutes, then drained
2 tbsp tahini
1 tsp vanilla bean paste or extract
pinch of sea salt
1 tsp apple cider vinegar
1 tsp ground or fresh turmeric

Chocolate ganache
100g dark chocolate, roughly
   chopped
⅓ cup coconut milk

Preheat the oven to 200°C. Line a baking tray with baking paper.

Slice the bananas, place on the baking tray, and bake for 20 minutes.

To make the brownie, place the walnuts and coconut into a blender or food processor, and blend into a coarse flour. Add the remaining brownie ingredients, and blend until well-combined and you have a dough that sticks together nicely.

Line a loaf tin with beeswax wraps or cling film. Place the brownie mixture into the tin, and press down evenly using the back of a spoon. Place in the freezer while you make the banana filling.

Your bananas should have finished roasting and be lovely and caramelised.

For the ice cream, place all of the ingredients, including the bananas, into the blender, and blend until super-smooth.

Take the base out of the freezer, and pour the banana ice cream over the top. Bang the tin a few times on the bench top to remove any air bubbles and get a smooth finish. Place back in the freezer to set for 3 hours.

Once the banana ice cream is set, you can make the chocolate ganache.

Melt the chocolate using a double boiler.

Once the chocolate is fully melted, pour in the coconut milk and whisk. The chocolate will become thicker and glossy. Pour the ganache over the banana ice cream, and give it a gentle shake from side to side to spread it over evenly. Place in the freezer for a further 30 minutes, to set.

Once the chocolate ganache is set, remove from the freezer and cut into slices. Store in an airtight container in the freezer, where they will keep for up to 3 months. (As dates don't actually freeze, this slice is great because it can be eaten straight out of the freezer.)

HAZELNUT BUTTER POPCORN CHOCOLATE TRUFFLES

Chocolate hazelnut spread, made into a cookie-dough form and rolled into a ball ...
  Chunks of chewy popcorn within the truffles give an exciting texture and make
for a tasty morsel to eat. Rolling them in more popcorn makes them look like little
planets. Kids will love them for birthday parties or as a sweet treat.

MAKES 10

Prep time: 20 minutes

½ cup dry-roasted
   hazelnuts or ½ cup
   hazelnut butter
¾ cup dates, softened
   in boiling water for
   5–10 minutes, then
   drained
⅓ cup cacao powder
pinch of sea salt
1 cup popcorn
cacao powder, to coat

Place the hazelnuts into a blender or food processor, and blend to a butter. (If you don't have a high-speed blender, you can still use hazelnuts but you won't get a super-smooth texture; or, alternatively, you can use hazelnut butter.)

Once you have a butter consistency, add the dates, cacao powder and salt. Blend until you have a smooth, chocolatey truffle mixture.

Place the mixture into a small bowl, and crush ½ cup of the popcorn into the bowl. Mix the popcorn into the chocolate mixture until it is well-combined. Roll the mixture into 1 tbsp balls.

Crush the remaining ½ cup of popcorn, and roll half of the balls in the popcorn, and the other half in cacao powder.

Store in an airtight container in the freezer, where they will keep for up to 2 months.

BANANA BOATS

Stuff bananas with chocolate — and 7 minutes later you are left with soft, caramelised banana flesh and melted chocolate everywhere. An effortless, cost-effective dessert to make during winter or on a summer's night by the campfire. We love serving it with salted caramel sauce, chopped roasted peanuts and ice cream.

SERVES 4

Prep time: 10 minutes
Cooking time: 7 minutes

4 ripe bananas
50g dark chocolate, roughly
  chopped

Caramel sauce
¾ cup coconut milk
½ cup dates, softened
  in boiling water for
  5–10 minutes, then
  drained
¼ tsp sea salt

To serve
coconut yoghurt or ice
  cream
goji berries
roasted peanuts, chopped
dark chocolate, roughly
  chopped

Preheat the oven to 200°C.

Leaving the banana skins on, cut the bananas clean down the middle. In each banana half, make a slit down the middle. Cut until you get to the skin, but *don't* cut through the skins. Stuff each banana half with chopped dark chocolate.

Place the bananas on a baking tray, and bake for 7 minutes.

While the bananas are cooking, make the caramel sauce. Place all of the ingredients into a blender, and blend until smooth and creamy. Set aside.

Once the bananas are cooked, place them on a plate and top them with caramel sauce, coconut yoghurt or ice cream, goji berries, peanuts and extra chocolate.

Eat immediately.

SALTED CHOCOLATE MOUSSE ICE CREAM

Frozen zucchini makes this instant ice cream super fluffy and light. We always add it into smoothies to bulk them up without adding lots of fruit. This mousse ice cream has a beautiful balance of salty, bitter and sweet flavours. Whether it's for breakfast or dessert, you will love this simple, instant ice cream.

SERVES 2–3

Prep time: 7 minutes

3 frozen bananas, chopped
  before freezing
1 frozen zucchini, chopped
  before freezing
¼ cup coconut milk
⅓ cup cacao powder
¼–½ tsp sea salt

½ cup dark chocolate, roughly
  chopped

Blend all of the ingredients, excluding the chocolate, in a blender or a food processor, until smooth and creamy.

Fold through the roughly chopped chocolate.

To serve, divide between bowls.

If you are not eating the ice cream immediately, put it in a metal tin and place in the freezer. Do not store it for longer than 2 hours, otherwise the ice cream will freeze and go hard.

CARAMEL SLICE

We have made a rule that this must be stocked in our freezer 24/7. The shortbread base is incredible with the thick layer of creamy caramel. The secret ingredient to our caramel is the tahini. Rather than just being a date caramel, the tahini adds a decadent depth of flavour and indulgence, making it a caramel slice like no other.

The addition of tahini to the chocolate means you are going to get a smooth cut. No more cracks ruining your amazing-looking caramel slice.

MAKES 12

Prep time: 35 minutes
Setting time: caramel
(1 hour) + once chocolate
is on (at least 3 hours)

Shortbread base
½ cup buckwheat or rolled
   oats
½ cup cashews
½ cup desiccated coconut
½ cup dates, softened
   in boiling water for
   5–10 minutes, then drained
2 tbsp coconut oil, melted
pinch of sea salt

Caramel
3 cups dates, softened in
   boiling water for
   5–10 minutes, then drained
1 cup cashews, softened in
   boiling water for
   5–10 minutes, then drained
½ cup coconut oil, melted
1 cup coconut milk
1 tbsp vanilla bean paste or
   extract
3 tbsp tahini
1–2 tsp sea salt

Chocolate topping
200g dark chocolate, roughly
   chopped
2 tbsp tahini

Place the buckwheat, cashews and coconut into a blender or food processor, and blend until a fine flour is formed. Add the remaining shortbread ingredients. Blend until you have a well-combined dough consistency.

Line a slice tin with beeswax wraps or baking paper. Evenly press the base into the bottom of the container. Smooth out with the back of a spoon. Set aside.

To make the caramel, blend all of the ingredients in the blender, until smooth and creamy. Pour it over the base, and bang the tin a few times on the bench top to remove any air bubbles and get a smooth finish. Place in the freezer for 1 hour, to set.

Once the caramel is set, make the chocolate topping. Melt the chocolate using a double boiler. Once melted, add in the tahini and mix until well-combined, and you have a smooth, glossy liquid. Pour it evenly over the caramel. Gently bang the tin against the bench top again to evenly spread the chocolate.

Place in the freezer for at least 3 hours, to set.

Once set, cut the caramel into slices.

Store the slices in an airtight container in the freezer, where they will keep for up to 3 months.

CARAMEL PEANUT BARS

These are our two favourite things combined into one: caramel slice and peanut butter. A base of vanilla shortbread, followed by a thick pour of salty caramel. Finish it off with a slab of peanut butter chocolate, chunky roasted peanuts and extra chocolate — because why not?! This slice 100% ticks all of the boxes.

MAKES 8

Prep time: 35 minutes
Setting time: 2–3 hours + 1–2 hours

Vanilla shortbread

1 cup buckwheat or rolled oats
½ cup pumpkin seeds
½ cup cashew butter
1 tsp vanilla bean paste or extract
2–3 tbsp 100% pure maple syrup
pinch of sea salt

Caramel

1½ cups dates, softened
  in boiling water for
  5–10 minutes, then drained
¼ cup cashews, softened
  in boiling water for
  5–10 minutes, then drained
⅓ cup coconut oil, melted
¼ cup coconut milk
2 tbsp tahini
1 tsp vanilla bean paste or extract
½ tsp sea salt

a handful of roasted peanuts,
  roughly chopped

Peanut butter chocolate

100g dark chocolate, roughly
  chopped
6 tbsp peanut butter
1 tbsp 100% pure maple syrup
1 tsp vanilla bean paste or extract
pinch of sea salt

To serve

dark chocolate, melted
roasted peanuts, roughly
  chopped

To make the shortbread, put the buckwheat and pumpkin seeds into a blender or food processor, and blend until a flour is formed. Add the remaining ingredients, and blend until you have a smooth shortbread dough.

Line a tin with beeswax wraps or cling film, and evenly press the shortbread dough into the tin. Flatten out with the back of a spoon. Set aside.

To make the caramel, place all of the ingredients, except the handful of roasted peanuts, into the blender or food processor, and blend until smooth.

Pour the caramel over the base. Bang the tin a few times on the bench top to get rid of any air bubbles and to get a smooth finish. Sprinkle over the chopped peanuts, and press them lightly into the caramel with your hand. Place the slice into the freezer for 2–3 hours, to set.

Once the caramel is set, make the peanut butter chocolate. Melt the dark chocolate using a double boiler. Once the chocolate has melted, add the remaining ingredients, and mix until the peanut butter has dissolved.

Take the caramel out of the freezer and evenly pour the peanut butter chocolate over the caramel, flattening it out with the back of a spoon. Place the caramel back into the freezer for a further 1–2 hours, to set.

Once everything is fully set, cut into bars, and drizzle with the melted chocolate and sprinkle with peanuts.

Store the bars in an airtight container in the freezer, where they will keep for up to 3 months.

PEANUT BUTTER BANANA SLICE

For all you peanut butter lovers out there, you will love these. Yes, it is quite a lot of peanut butter, but trust us, it is worth it. Bananas are a cost-effective filler for the filling, and give a natural sweetness. We would be lying if we said we didn't have this for breakfast on the odd occasion ...

MAKES 10

Prep time: 25 minutes
Setting time: 3–4 hours

Base
1 cup walnuts or
　rolled oats
1 cup desiccated
　coconut
½ cup dates,
　softened in
　boiling water for
　5–10 minutes,
　then drained
2 tbsp cacao powder
pinch of sea salt

Filling
4 ripe bananas
1½ cups peanut
　butter
4 tbsp coconut oil,
　melted
pinch of sea salt
¼ cup cacao powder

To make the base, place the walnuts and coconut into a blender or food processor, and blend until you have a fine flour. Add the remaining ingredients to the blender, and blend until you have a smooth dough that sticks together nicely. If it is too crumbly, add 1–2 tablespoons of water.

Line a loaf tin with beeswax wraps or baking paper. Press the base evenly into the tin, using the back of a spoon. Set aside.

To make the filling, place the bananas, peanut butter, 2 tablespoons of coconut oil and a pinch of salt in the blender or food processor. Blend until you have a thick, creamy mixture.

Pour half of the mixture onto the base, and flatten with the back of a spoon. Place the slice in the freezer for 1 hour, to set.

While the first layer is setting, start making the second layer. Add the cacao and 2 tablespoons of coconut oil to the remaining mixture, and blend until well-combined.

Once the first layer is set, pour the chocolate mixture on top of the first layer, flattening with a spoon once more. Place the slice back into the freezer for another 2–3 hours, to fully set.

Once the entire slice is set, remove it from the tin and cut into slices.

Store the slices in an airtight container in the freezer, where they will keep for up to 3 months. When you are wanting to eat a slice, allow about 10–15 minutes for it to thaw.

SALTED ROASTED BANANA CARAMEL SLICE

Roasting bananas gives them the most amazing depth of flavour, and makes them taste a bit like a banana milkshake.

This is a nice change from a caramel- or chocolate-based slice, which can be quite rich for some people. Give this one a go: it is one of our top favourites.

MAKES 10

Prep time: 25 minutes
Cooking time: 10 minutes
Setting time: 2 hours

Shortbread base
½ cup buckwheat or
    rolled oats
½ cup cashews
½ cup coconut flour
½ cup dates, softened
    in boiling water for
    5–10 minutes, then drained
2 tbsp water (add more if
    needed)
juice of ½ lemon or
    ½ tsp apple cider vinegar
pinch of sea salt

Caramel
3 ripe bananas
¾ cup coconut milk
¼ cup coconut oil, melted
½ cup cashews, softened
    in boiling water for
    5–10 minutes, then drained
½ cup dates, softened
    in boiling water for
    5–10 minutes, then drained
2 tbsp tahini
1 tsp vanilla bean paste or
    extract
1 tsp sea salt
1 tsp apple cider vinegar

Preheat the oven to 200°C.

To make the shortbread base, place the buckwheat and cashews into a blender or food processor, and blend until a flour is formed. Add the remaining ingredients, and blend until you have a well-combined dough. Line a loaf tin with beeswax wraps or cling film. Press the base evenly into the loaf tin, using the back of a spoon. Set aside.

To make the caramel, cut the bananas into discs, place them on a lined baking tray, and put them in the oven for 10 minutes.

Once the bananas are caramelised and smelling sweet, bring them out, and place them into the blender or food processor, along with the remaining ingredients. Blend until smooth.

Pour the caramel evenly over the base, banging the tin on the bench top a couple of times to get rid of any air bubbles and get a smooth finish. Place in the freezer for 2 hours, to set.

Once set, remove from the freezer, and cut into slices.

Store the slices in an airtight container in the freezer, where they will keep for up to 2 months. When you are wanting to eat a slice, allow about 10–15 minutes for it to thaw.

PASSIONFRUIT SLICE

Passionfruit and honey are a match made in heaven. This recipe is a life hack for anyone who doesn't have a high-speed blender like a Vitamix. Rather than using raw cashews and being left with a gritty texture, we have used cashew butter. This means that all of the tough blending has been done for you, and, no matter what type of equipment you have, the filling will always be super-smooth and creamy.

MAKES 10

Prep time: 25 minutes
Setting time: 2 hours

Base
¾ cup dried coconut
½ cup almonds
½ cup buckwheat or rolled oats
¾ cup dates, softened in boiling water for 5–10 minutes, then drained
2 tbsp coconut oil, melted
1 tsp ground ginger
½ tsp vanilla bean paste or extract
pinch of sea salt

Filling
½ cup cashew butter
1 overripe banana
3 tbsp coconut oil, melted
2 tbsp honey
½ tsp vanilla bean paste or extract
pinch of sea salt

pulp of 3 passionfruit

To serve
coconut yoghurt
pulp of 1 passionfruit
drizzle of honey

To make the base, place the coconut, almonds and buckwheat into a blender or food processor, and blend until you have a rough flour. Add the remaining ingredients, and blend until you have a cookie-dough consistency.

Line a tart tin with beeswax wraps or cling film, and press the base into the tin, using the back of a spoon. Press the mixture up the sides to create a crust. Set aside.

To make the filling, place all of the ingredients, except for the passionfruit pulp, into the blender or food processor, and blend until smooth.

Pour the filling over the base, and bang the tin on the bench top a couple of times to get rid of any air bubbles and get a smooth finish.

Spoon the passionfruit pulp over the filling, and with the handle of a spoon or a wooden skewer gently make a ripple effect. Place the slice in the freezer for 2 hours, to set.

Once the slice is set, remove it from the freezer, and top it with coconut yoghurt, passionfruit, and a drizzle of honey. Cut it into slices and enjoy.

Store the slices in an airtight container in the freezer, where they will keep for up to 4 months. When you are wanting to eat a slice, allow about 10–15 minutes for it to thaw.

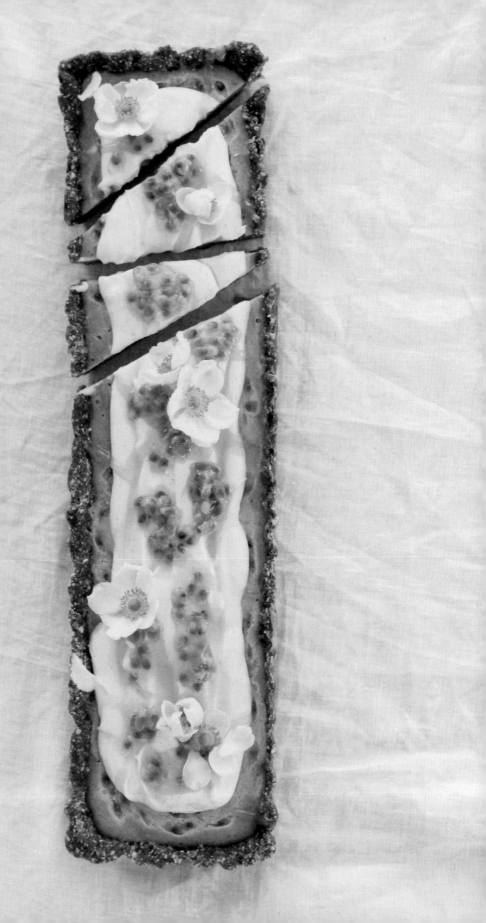

BANANA CAKE

This is our favourite afternoon treat before a workshop, or as a dessert with a scoop of ice cream. It satisfies all of the cravings for something sweet, nourishing, filling and decadent. The avocado chocolate icing is the best icing we have ever eaten. The great thing about this cake is that it lasts a good week, and develops in flavour over time. P.S.: If you eat eggs, then feel free to use 2 eggs instead of our suggested flax 'eggs'.

SERVES 8–10

Prep time: 25 minutes
Cooking time: 40 minutes
Setting time: 20–30 minutes

Dry ingredients
2 cups buckwheat or rolled oats
½ cup coconut sugar
2 tsp baking powder
½ tsp baking soda
1 tsp ground cinnamon
1 tsp ground ginger
pinch of sea salt

Wet ingredients
2 flax 'eggs' (2 tbsp ground flaxseed
    mixed with 6 tbsp water)
4 ripe bananas, mashed
¼ cup tahini
¼ cup coconut oil, melted
2 tbsp apple cider vinegar
1 tsp vanilla bean paste or extract
½ cup oat or nut milk

Chocolate icing
1 avocado
1 tbsp coconut oil
50g dark chocolate, roughly chopped
1 tbsp cacao powder, plus extra to serve
1 tbsp 100% pure maple syrup or honey
pinch of sea salt

continued ...

Preheat the oven to 180°C. Line the bottom of a cake tin with baking paper, and rub the sides with melted coconut oil. Set aside.

Place the buckwheat into a blender or food processor, and blend into a flour. Transfer to a large bowl, along with the rest of the dry ingredients. Mix until well-combined.

In another bowl, place all of the wet ingredients, and mix until everything is well-combined.

Add the wet ingredients to the dry ingredients, and fold the mixture until everything is combined.

Pour the cake mix into the lined cake tin. Place in the oven, and cook for 40 minutes.

While the cake is cooking, make the chocolate icing.

Put the avocado flesh into the blender. Set aside.

Melt the coconut oil and dark chocolate using a double boiler. Add the cacao, maple and salt, and mix to combine. Pour into the blender with the avocado, and gently blitz until a smooth chocolate mix is formed.

Place the icing into a bowl, and put it in the fridge, to harden up.

Once the cake is cooked, remove it from the tin and place it onto a cooling rack. Allow to cool completely before icing.

Once the cake has cooled, remove the icing from the fridge, and spread it evenly over the cake. To serve, dust with extra cacao powder.

Store this cake in an airtight container in your fridge, where it will keep for up to 7 days.

NUT-FREE AVOCADO CHOCOLATE TART

This nut-free tart is very decadent, and has the most divine mousse-like consistency thanks to the creamy mix of avocado and dark chocolate. Spiked with a delicate flavour of sweet honey, this tart is perfect for entertaining a crowd or anyone with nut allergies. The activated buckwheat is optional; however, it does add a lovely crunchy texture to the smoothness of the tart.

The base is a super-simple raw banana bread, using only 5 ingredients. We often find ourselves adding a couple of tablespoons of honey and rolling it into bliss balls for snacks.

SERVES 10

Prep time: 25 minutes
Setting time: 1–2 hours

Base
2 cups buckwheat or
    rolled oats
½ cup cacao powder
2 ripe bananas
1 tbsp honey
pinch of sea salt

Filling
100g dark chocolate,
    roughly chopped
¼ cup coconut oil
1 avocado
½ cup milk
¼ cup coconut oil
4 tbsp honey
pinch of sea salt

Topping
⅓ cup activated
    buckwheat
    (optional)

Place the buckwheat into a blender or food processor, and blend into a fine flour. Add the remaining base ingredients, and blend until you have a dense dough.

Line a cake tin with beeswax wraps or cling film. Press the dough right up the sides, and evenly over the entire base. Set aside.

To make the filling, melt the chocolate and coconut oil using a double boiler.

Place the remaining filling ingredients into the blender. Once the chocolate is melted, pour it into the blender as well. Blend until you have a smooth, glossy mixture.

Pour the filling over the base, and bang the tin a few times on your bench top to remove any air bubbles and get a smooth finish. Sprinkle over the activated buckwheat, if using.

Place the tart in the freezer for 1–2 hours, to set.

Once set, remove the tart from the freezer, and cut into slices. Serve with coconut yoghurt or ice cream.

Store in the fridge in an airtight container, where it will keep for up to 7 days, or in the freezer for up to 2 months. If stored in the freezer, allow about 10–15 minutes for the tart to thaw before you eat it.

CARROT CAKE

Carrot cake is an all-time favourite of ours, and this raw version is so much easier and faster than the traditional version.

The cake features earthy walnuts blended with sweet caramel dates, is spiked with beautiful, warming autumn spices and fresh orange, and is topped with the simplest, most delicious 4-ingredient vanilla orange cream. Made in 10 minutes, and using everyday pantry ingredients, how much easier can it get?!

SERVES 8

Prep time: 25 minutes
Setting time: 2 hours

1 heaped cup walnuts, plus ¼ cup walnuts, roughly chopped
1 cup oats
1½ cups dates, softened in boiling water for 5–10 minutes, then drained
4 small carrots, grated
2 tbsp ground flaxseed
1 tbsp fresh ginger, grated
1 tbsp ground cinnamon
1 tsp ground turmeric
juice of ½ orange
pinch of sea salt

Vanilla orange cream
2 cups thick coconut yoghurt
zest of 1 orange
1 tbsp 100% pure maple syrup
½ tsp vanilla bean paste or extract

Toppings
walnuts, chopped
pumpkin seeds
dried apricots, diced

Place the first measure of walnuts and the oats into a blender or food processor, and blend until you have a fine flour. Add the remaining ingredients, except the second measure of walnuts, and blend until you have a smooth, doughy mixture. Mix through the remaining measure of walnuts, until well-combined.

Line a cake tin with beeswax wraps or cling film, and press the cake mixture into the tin, spreading evenly with the back of a spoon. Place the cake in the freezer for at least 2 hours, to set.

While the cake is setting, make the vanilla orange cream. Place all of the ingredients in a bowl, and mix until well-combined. The cream can be made in advance and stored in the fridge, where it will keep for up to 2 weeks.

Once the cake is set, take it out of the freezer. Spread the cream over the top of the cake, and sprinkle with walnuts, pumpkin seeds and dried apricots.

Store in the fridge in an airtight container, where it will keep for up to 1 week, or in the freezer, where it will keep for up to 1 month.

If storing in the freezer, omit the cream and dollop it on fresh when serving. Allow the cake to thaw for about 10–15 minutes before you serve it.

SKILLET-ROASTED BANANA CRUMBLE

Everyone makes apple crumble; it is so yesterday. Instead, try our nifty new banana version. It is so easy, and uses only a skillet pan – so minimal dishes involved. If you don't have a skillet, a baking dish will work just as well. There is plenty of delicious crumble to go around, made from walnuts, pumpkin seeds and warming spices, and bound by the banana. Serve with a dollop of yoghurt or your favourite ice cream.

SERVES 4–6

Prep time: 15 minutes
Cooking time: 25 minutes

4 ripe bananas

Crumble
6 tbsp quinoa flakes or
    rolled oats
3 tbsp coconut flour
2 tbsp pumpkin seeds
¼ cup walnuts
½ banana, mashed
1 tbsp coconut oil, melted
1 tsp ground cinnamon
1 tsp ground ginger
1 tsp apple cider vinegar
pinch of sea salt
1 tbsp coconut sugar
¼ cup dark chocolate,
    roughly chopped

Preheat the oven to 180°C.

Grease a 22cm skillet, rubbing on coconut oil with a paper towel.

Slice the bananas lengthways, and peel the skins off. Tightly pack them together on the bottom of the skillet, and place in the oven for 10 minutes.

While the bananas are cooking, make the crumble. Place all of the crumble ingredients into a bowl, and mix until you have achieved a crumbly cookie-dough-like consistency.

Take the semi-cooked bananas out of the oven, and top with the crumble. Place back in the oven for 15 minutes, or until the crumble is lovely and golden.

This is great served with ice cream and extra chopped chocolate.

Store any leftovers in an airtight container in the fridge, where they will keep for up to 2–3 days.

DARK CHOCOLATE GINGER PEANUT SKILLET COOKIE

One giant cookie, designed to be eaten around a table with ice cream and shared by many. Spicy ginger cookie dough with peanut butter and melted chocolate all over! It doesn't get any more comforting than this.

If you prefer, you can make this into normal cookie sizes and have them as snacks.

SERVES 4–6

Prep time: 15 minutes
Cooking time: 12 minutes
Cooling time: 10 minutes

Dry ingredients
1 cup buckwheat or
    rolled oats
2 tsp ground ginger
¼ tsp baking soda

Wet ingredients
¼ cup peanut butter
2 tbsp coconut sugar
2 tbsp 100% pure
    maple syrup
4 tbsp coconut oil,
    melted
2 tbsp water

Topping
2 tbsp peanut butter
¼ cup roughly
    chopped dark
    chocolate
handful of peanuts,
    roasted and roughly
    chopped

Preheat the oven to 180°C. Grease a 20cm cast-iron skillet (or cake tin) by rubbing on coconut oil with a paper towel. Set aside.

Place the buckwheat into a blender or food processor, and blend into a flour. Transfer into a bowl, along with the rest of the dry ingredients. Mix until well-combined, and then set aside.

Place all of the wet ingredients into a small bowl, and mix until you have a well-combined, thick mixture. Pour the wet ingredients in with the dry ingredients, and mix until well-combined.

Press the dough evenly onto the prepared skillet (it should be about 1cm thick). Add a few tablespoons of peanut butter on top of the dough, as well as the dark chocolate and peanuts.

Bake in the oven for 12 minutes, or until the edges are slightly golden. Do not over-bake, as this cookie is better when the centre is a little underdone. Remove from the oven, and let cool for 10 minutes.

Eat straight from the pan with spoons. It's great served with ice cream or coconut yoghurt.

Store any leftovers in an airtight container in the fridge, where they will keep for 10 days.

PEANUT BUTTER AQUAFABA MOUSSE

Aquafaba is the brine from a can of chickpeas. Weird, we know, but it creates the most luscious fluffy mousse you will ever eat. The vinegar is essential, as it helps hold the fluffiness. We learnt that the hard way ...

SERVES 4

Prep time: 30 minutes
Setting time: 8 hours +
15 minutes

Mousse
½ cup smooth
   peanut butter
3 tbsp coconut milk
1 tbsp honey
pinch of sea salt
brine in 1 x 400g can
   of chickpeas (this
   is the aquafaba)
½ tsp apple cider
   vinegar

Quick chocolate ganache
80g dark chocolate,
   roughly chopped
¼ cup nut or oat milk

Place the peanut butter, coconut milk, honey and salt into a bowl, and whisk until you have a thick, smooth mixture.

Drain the brine of the can of chickpeas (this is the aquafaba) into a medium-sized bowl, and add the vinegar. Using a clean electric beater, whip the aquafaba until you have stiff peaks. (It should resemble whipped cream.)

Add one-third of the whipped aquafaba to the peanut butter mixture, and fold it through until well-combined. Because the peanut butter mixture is quite thick, you have to fold it a lot this first-time round. The mixture will deflate a fair bit, but don't worry — this is why we add in only a little bit now! Add the rest of the whipped aquafaba, and fold it very gently, as you don't want to knock too much air out while mixing.

Divide the mixture between 4 small glasses, and place them in the fridge for 8 hours, or overnight, to allow the mousse to set.

To make the ganache, melt the chocolate using a double boiler. When the chocolate is melted, add the milk, and whisk until you have a thick, smooth chocolate. Divide between the 4 glasses, and tilt the glasses in circles until the ganache is evenly spread on the top and around the edges.

Place in the freezer for 15 minutes to set the ganache.

Once set, eat straight out of the freezer or store in the fridge, where it will keep for up to 1 week.

APPLE WALNUT PIE

This is our version of a revamped apple crumble. It has a thick peanut butter cake-like layer stuffed with chunks of apple. This is followed by a generous sprinkle of caramelised walnut crumble, and served with vanilla bean ice cream. It is totally delicious to eat snuggled up by the fire on a winter's night. Leftovers are great for breakfast.

SERVES 4–6

Prep time: 20 minutes
Cooking time: 20 minutes

Pie
3 ripe bananas, mashed
½ cup smooth peanut
    butter
1½ cups oats (or brown
    rice flakes, buckwheat
    flakes or quinoa flakes)
1 apple, cut into 2cm
    cubes
pinch of salt

Crumble
½ cup walnuts, roughly
    chopped
½ cup raisins
¼ cup coconut flakes
pinch of sea salt
1 tbsp honey
1 tbsp coconut oil, melted

Preheat the oven to 180°C. Line an ovenproof dish with baking paper, and set aside.

To make the pie, place the mashed bananas, peanut butter, oats, apple and salt into a medium-sized bowl, and mix together. Pour into the lined dish, and place in the oven to bake for 15 minutes.

While the pie is cooking, make the crumble topping. In a small bowl mix the walnuts, raisins, coconut flakes and salt. Pour over the honey and coconut oil, and toss until the crumble is well-coated.

Once the pie is cooked, evenly sprinkle the topping over the pie, and lightly press it into the pie mixture with the palm of your hand. Place back in the oven for 5 minutes, until the walnuts and coconut become golden brown.

Divide the walnut pie onto plates, and top with a dollop of coconut yoghurt or ice cream.

Store any leftovers in an airtight container in the fridge, where they will keep for 5 days.

PB CHOCOLATE MAGIC SHELL

This makes vanilla ice cream out of this world. It is so easy to make, and the kids (and adults) will love seeing it harden into a shell before their eyes. You can also use it as a chocolate top on slices and snack bars.

SERVES 3–4

Prep time: 7 minutes

50g dark chocolate, roughly chopped
1 tbsp coconut oil
¼ cup roasted peanuts, finely chopped
1 tbsp smooth peanut butter
1 tbsp coconut oil

Melt the dark chocolate and coconut oil using a double boiler.

Once the chocolate is melted, add the remaining ingredients, and mix until well-combined.

Spoon the chocolate shell over ice cream, or you can also use this shell to top a slice, such as our Caramel Slice (see page 178).

This can be stored in the freezer in an airtight container, where it will keep for up to 2 months, and can be re-melted when needed.

CHOCOLATE TART WITH TAHINI SALTED CARAMEL

Such a decadent, indulgent tart. An earthy walnut base paired with an incredibly silky-smooth chocolate filling of dark chocolate, tahini and coconut milk. The coconut whip helps mellow out the richness, and the salted caramel rounds everything off beautifully. This is a great one to make when you want to impress some guests, or just when you need a slice of deep, cosy comfort.

SERVES 12

Prep time: 40 minutes
Setting time: 2 hours

Base
1 cup walnuts
½ cup buckwheat or rolled
  oats
½ cup dates, softened
  in boiling water for
  5–10 minutes, then drained
¼ cup cacao powder
1 tsp vanilla bean paste
  or extract
pinch of sea salt

Chocolate filling
200g dark chocolate, roughly
  chopped
½ cup tahini
1 cup coconut milk
3 tbsp maple or honey
½ tsp sea salt

Caramel
1 cup dates, softened
  in boiling water for
  5–10 minutes, then drained
¼–½ cup coconut milk
2 tbsp tahini
1 tsp vanilla bean paste or
  extract
¼ tsp sea salt

Coconut whip
1 cup coconut yoghurt
1 tsp vanilla bean paste or
  extract

To serve
dark chocolate, roughly
  chopped

To make the base, line a tart tin with beeswax wraps or cling film, and set aside. Place the walnuts and buckwheat into a blender or food processor. Blend into a fine flour. Add the remaining base ingredients, and blend until you have a smooth cookie-dough consistency. Transfer the base into the lined tin, and evenly press up the sides and on the bottom, using the back of a spoon to flatten it. Set the base aside.

To make the filling, melt the dark chocolate using a double boiler. Once the chocolate has melted, add the remaining ingredients for the chocolate filling, and whisk until you have a shiny, thick, smooth liquid. Pour the filling over the base, and bang the tin on the bench top a couple of time to get rid of any air bubbles and get a smooth finish. Place in the freezer for 2 hours, to set.

While the filling is setting, make the caramel. Simply put all of the ingredients into the blender or food processor, and blend until you have a smooth caramel. Set aside.

To make the coconut whip, place the coconut yoghurt into a bowl, and mix in the vanilla bean paste or extract until well-combined. Set aside.

When the tart is set, take it out of the freezer. Spread the coconut whip over the top, using the back of a spoon to spread it out. Then drizzle the caramel over the coconut whip — we like to serve some extra caramel on the side, too. Lastly, sprinkle with roughly chopped chocolate.

Serve immediately, or store in an airtight container in the fridge, where it will keep for up to 7 days.

INDEX